SCIENCE FuSiOn

fusion [FYOO • zhuhn] a combination of two or more things that releases energy

This Write-In Student Edition belongs to

_____

Teacher/Room

_____

 HOUGHTON MIFFLIN HARCOURT

HOUGHTON MIFFLIN HARCOURT

Front Cover: *anole* ©Jeremy Woodhouse/Photodisc/Getty Images; *prism* ©Larry Lilac/Alamy; *clownfish* ©Georgette Douwma/Photographer's Choice/Getty Images; *galaxy* ©Stocktrek/Corbis; *fern* ©Mauro Fermariello/Photo Researchers Inc.

Back Cover: *moth* ©Millard H. Sharp/Photo Researchers Inc.; *astronaut* ©NASA; *thermometer* ©Stockimages/Alamy; *gear* ©Garry Gay/The Image Bank/Getty Images.

Consulting Authors

Michael A. DiSpezio
Global Educator
North Falmouth, Massachusetts

Marjorie Frank
Science Writer and Content-Area Reading
   Specialist
Brooklyn, New York

Michael R. Heithaus
Director, School of Environment and Society
Associate Professor, Department of Biological
   Sciences
Florida International University
North Miami, Florida

Donna M. Ogle
Professor of Reading and Language
National-Louis University
Chicago, Illinois

Program Advisors

Paul D. Asimow
Professor of Geology and
   Geochemistry
California Institute of Technology
Pasadena, California

Bobby Jeanpierre
Associate Professor of Science
   Education
University of Central Florida
Orlando, Florida

Gerald H. Krockover
Professor of Earth and Atmospheric
   Science Education
Purdue University
West Lafayette, Indiana

Rose Pringle
Associate Professor
School of Teaching and Learning
College of Education
University of Florida
Gainesville, Florida

Carolyn Staudt
Curriculum Designer for Technology
KidSolve, Inc.
The Concord Consortium
Concord, Massachusetts

Larry Stookey
Science Department
Antigo High School
Antigo, Wisconsin

Carol J. Valenta
Associate Director of the Museum and
   Senior Vice President
Saint Louis Science Center
St. Louis, Missouri

Barry A. Van Deman
President and CEO
Museum of Life and Science
Durham, North Carolina

Power Up with Science Fusion!

Your program fuses . . .

e-Learning & Virtual Labs

Labs & Explorations

Write-In Student Edition

. . . to generate new science energy for today's science learner— you.

Write-In Student Edition

Be an active reader and make this book your own!

Write your ideas, answer questions, make notes, and record activity results right on these pages.

Learn science concepts and skills by interacting with every page.

Amphibians or Rep...

How are amphibians and reptiles differen...
Read on to learn about these two groups.

...tive Reading As you read these two pages, draw circles around
t... ...ve words that signal when things are being compared.

Amphibians [am•FIB•ee•...

...the tadpoles look like fish. Most
amphibians have smooth, moist
...kin. Young amphibians have gills.
...ny adult amphibians have lungs.
...ptiles are animals with scales
cov...ng their bodies. Lizards
and tu...les are reptiles. Similar to
amphibia...s, most reptiles hat...
from eggs. A reptile h...
lungs its wh...
crocodiles, th...
water must c...

...amphibian li...round water.

...tle

...R

...eptile lays eggs.

Newts la...
water.

**Frille...
Lizar...**

**Frilled lizard...
lay their eggs...
the ground.**

Labs & Activities

Science is all about doing.

Exciting investigations for every lesson.

Ask questions and test your ideas.

Draw conclusions and share what you learn.

How Can You Use a Model?

Have you ever wondered why a plane can fly? Since a real plane is too big for you to investigate, a model is the next best thing. In this activity, you will make and test a model airplane.

Materials
sheets of paper
tape
meterstick
safety goggles

1. Make your model airplane, following tips from your teacher.

2. CAUTION: Wear goggles when testing your model airplane! Fly your airplane in a place your teacher tells you is safe. Have a partner use the meterstick to measure how far the plane flies each time you throw it.

3. Ask yourself "How can I make the plane go farther?"

4. Write a hypothesis about what kinds of changes would work. For example, you might use a different kind of paper.

5. Test your hypothesis by changing your plane and measuring the distance it flies.

A Word for the Wise
When you test a **hypothesis**, you change only one thing at a time. That one thing is called the **variable**.

e-Learning & Virtual Labs

Digital lessons and virtual labs provide e-learning options for every lesson of *ScienceFusion*.

Let's do it!

Click the Reset button and run the experiment again if you missed anything.

Volume is a measure of how much space matter takes up.
By looking at these ice cubes, it is clear how much space they take up.

Use the camera to take a photo of water particles in the gas state.
Click the Reset button and run the experiment again if you missed anything.

On your own or with a group, explore science concepts in a digital world.

360° of Inquiry

Contents

Levels of Inquiry Key ▨ DIRECTED ▮ GUIDED ▨ INDEPENDENT

THE NATURE OF SCIENCE AND S.T.E.M.

LIFE SCIENCE

PHYSICAL SCIENCE

Investigating Questions

Big Idea

Scientists raise questions about Earth and the universe and seek answers to some of them by careful investigation.

Naples, Florida

I Wonder Why

Scientists work on the beach as well as many other places. How do scientists help animals survive? *Turn the page to find out.*

Here's why Scientists get their hands dirty! They use tools such as tags, cameras, notes, and maps to help animals survive.

In this unit, you will explore the Big Idea, the Essential Questions, and the Investigations on the Inquiry Flipchart.

Levels of Inquiry Key ■ DIRECTED ■ GUIDED ■ INDEPENDENT

Track Your Progress

Big Idea Scientists raise questions about Earth and the universe and seek answers to some of them by careful investigation.

Essential Questions

Now I Get the Big Idea!

Science Notebook
Before you begin each lesson, be sure to write your thoughts about the Essential Question.

Essential Question

How Do Scientists Investigate Questions?

 Engage Your Brain!

Find the answer to the following question in this lesson and record it here.

How is this student acting like a scientist?

_____

_____

_____

Active Reading

Lesson Vocabulary

List each term. As you learn about each, make notes in the Interactive Glossary.

_____ _____

_____ _____

_____ _____

_____

Use Headings

Active readers preview, or read, the headings first. Headings give the reader an idea of what the reading is about. Reading with a purpose helps active readers understand what they are reading.

What Is Science?

Science is about Earth and everything beyond it. What does a scientist look like? To find out, take a look in the mirror!

Active Reading As you read these two pages, underline the main idea.

Why do volcanoes erupt?

Look for a Question

How does a butterfly use its six legs? What does the shape of a cloud tell about the weather? It's never too soon to start asking questions! Write your own question below.

_____

_____

4

Science is a way of looking at the world and thinking about it. When you think like a scientist, you ask questions about the world around you. You try to answer your questions by doing investigations.

Some investigations are simple, such as watching animals play. Other investigations take planning. You need to gather and set up materials. Then you write down what happens.

You can think like a scientist on your own or in a group. Sharing what you learn is part of the fun. So get started!

Why does a compass point north?

What do stars look like through a telescope?

What Do You See?

So you want to think like a scientist? Let's get started. Try making some observations and inferences!

Active Reading As you read these two pages, find and underline the definition of *observe*.

Look at the pictures on this page. What do you see? When you use your senses to notice details, you **observe**.

Things you observe can start you thinking. Look at the picture of the small sailboat. You see that it has more than one sail. Now look more closely. The sails are different shapes and sizes.

You might infer that the shape or size of the sails affects how the boat moves. When you **infer**, you offer an explanation of what you observed. You might infer that each sail helps the boat move in a different way.

Make an observation about this boat.

_____

_____

_____

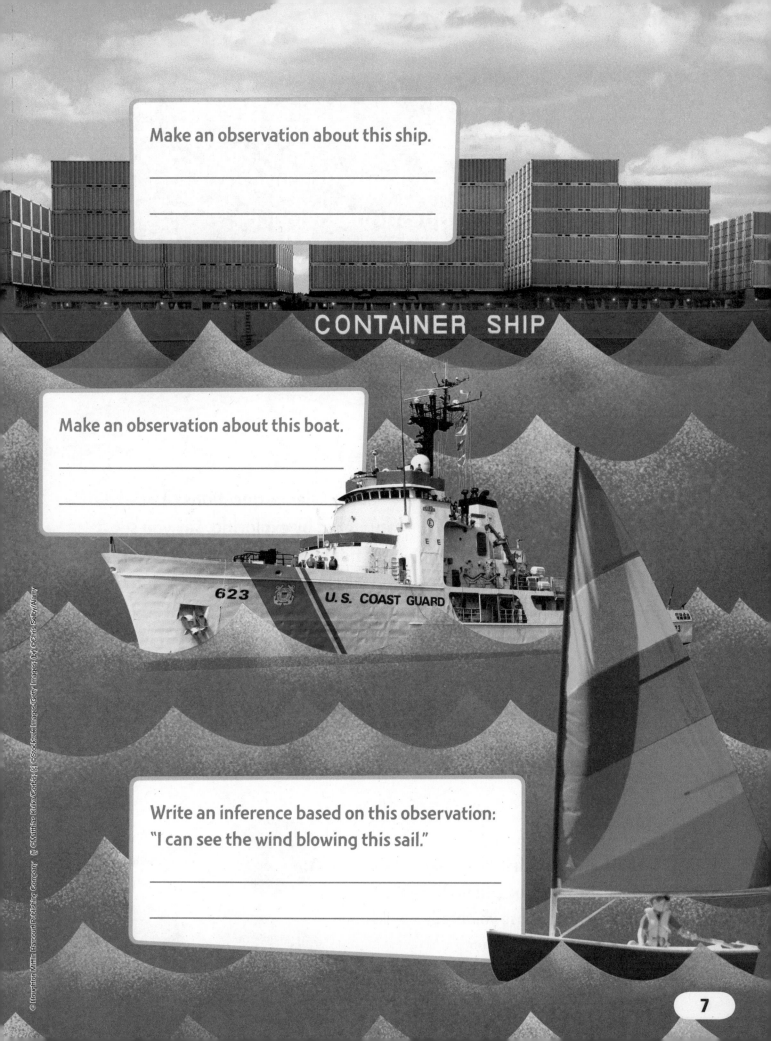

Make an observation about this ship.

_____

_____

CONTAINER SHIP

Make an observation about this boat.

_____

_____

623   U.S. COAST GUARD

Write an inference based on this observation:
"I can see the wind blowing this sail."

_____

_____

Getting Answers!

People ask questions all day long. But not all questions are science questions. Science questions can be answered in many ways.

Active Reading As you read these two pages, circle a common, everyday word that has a different meaning in science.

Exploring

Some science questions can be answered by exploring. Say you see a leaf float by on the water. You wonder what else can float on water. You find an eraser in your pocket. You **predict**, or use what you know to tell if it will sink or float. When you know which items float and which don't, you can **classify**, or group, them.

Predict

Think about each item pictured. Then circle the ones you predict will float. Mark an X on those you predict will sink.

Investigating

You might think of an investigation as looking for clues. In science, an **investigation** is a planned way of finding answers to questions. When you do an investigation, you might ask a cause-and-effect question, "Does the amount of weight in a boat affect whether it floats or sinks?" Because you don't want to use a real boat, you can **make and use models.** A raft made of sticks is not exactly like a real boat, but it can be used to learn about them.

Investigating Answers

There are many steps a scientist may take during an investigation. Some do all five described here.

Active Reading As you read these two pages, number the sentences that describe Onisha's experiment to match the numbered steps in the circles.

1 Ask a Question

What causes things to change? This is the kind of question you can answer with an investigation.

2 Hypothesize

A **hypothesis** is a statement that could answer your question. You must be able to test a hypothesis.

Predict and Plan an Investigation

Predict what you will observe if your hypothesis is correct. **Identify the variable** to test, and keep other variables the same.

3

What Onisha Did ...

Onisha thought about rafts floating down a river. She asked a question, "Does the size of a raft affect the amount of weight it can carry?"

Onisha **hypothesizes** that a bigger raft can carry more weight. Then she predicted, "I should be able to add more weight to a bigger raft than to a smaller raft." Onisha planned an investigation called an experiment. Outside of science, experimenting means trying something new, such as a new recipe. In science, an **experiment** is a test done to gather evidence. The evidence might support the hypothesis, or it might not. In her experiment, Onisha built three model rafts that differed only in their number of planks. She carefully put one penny at a time onto each raft until it sank. She recorded her results and drew a conclusion.

Variable

The factor that is changed in an experiment is called a **variable**. It's important to change only one variable at a time.

Draw Conclusions

Analyze your results, and **draw a conclusion.** Ask yourself, "Do the results support my hypothesis?" Share your conclusion with others.

4

Experiment

Now do the experiment to test your hypothesis.

5

▶ What was the variable in Onisha's experiment?

_____

_____

Sum It Up!

When you're done, use the answer key to check and revise your work.

Write words from the lesson that match the pictures.

1 _____

2 _____

3 _____

The small plane will fly farther.

4 _____

Use what you learned from the lesson to fill in the sequence below.

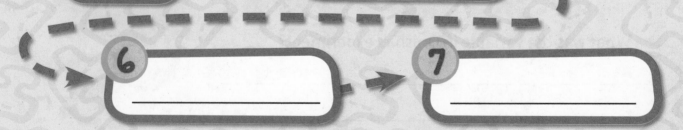

observe → **5** _____

6 _____ → **7** _____

Answer Key: 1. use models 2. variable 3. investigate 4. predict 5. infer 6. hypothesize 7. experiment

Word Play

Name _____

1. Use the words in the box to complete the puzzle.

Across

1. You do this when you make a conclusion after observing.

5. the one factor you change in an experiment

6. to make a guess based on what you know or think

8. something that is like the real thing—but not exactly

9. a statement that will answer a question you want to investigate

Down

1. Scientists plan and carry one out to answer their questions.

2. Scientists ask these about the world around them.

3. You do this when you use your five senses.

4. an investigation in which you use variables

7. You draw this at the end of an investigation.

experiment*   infer*   **questions**   investigation*   variable*   hypothesis*

predict*   **model**   observe*   **conclusion**

* Key Lesson Vocabulary

Apply Concepts

2 This bridge is over the Mississippi River. List materials you could use to make a model of it.

_____

_____

3 Greyson wants to know what plants need in order to survive. He places one plant in a window. He places another plant in a dark closet. What is the variable he is testing?

_____

4 Jared looks carefully at a young turtle in his hand. Label each of his statements _observation_ or _inference_.

Its front legs are longer than its back legs. _____

It has sharp toenails. _____

It uses its toenails to dig. _____

It can see me. _____

Its shell feels cool and dry against

my hand. _____

Take It Home! Share what you have learned about observations and inferences with your family. With a family member, make observations and inferences about items in or near your home.

Name _____

How Can You Use a Model?

Set a Purpose
What is the question you will try to answer with this investigation?

_____

_____

_____

State Your Hypothesis
Write your hypothesis, or idea you will test.

_____

_____

_____

Think About the Procedure
What is the variable you plan to test?

_____

_____

How will you know whether the variable you changed worked?

_____

_____

_____

Record Your Results
Fill in the chart to record how far the plane flew each time you changed its design.

Change Made to the Model	Distance It Flew

Draw Conclusions

1. Which changes to your model worked best?

_____

_____

_____

_____

2. Was your hypothesis supported by the results? How do you know?

_____

_____

_____

Analyze and Extend

1. How is your model the same as a real airplane?

_____

_____

_____

2. What did you learn about real airplanes from using a model?

_____

_____

_____

3. How is your model different from a real airplane?

_____

_____

_____

_____

4. What can't you learn about real airplanes by using a paper airplane?

_____

_____

_____

_____

_____

5. Think of another question you would like to answer about airplane models.

_____

_____

_____

_____

16

Essential Question

How Do Scientists Use Tools?

Engage Your Brain!

A hand lens can make a bug look bigger.

What other tools make objects look bigger?

_____

_____

_____

Active Reading

Lesson Vocabulary

List each term. As you learn about each one, make notes in the Interactive Glossary.

_____

_____

_____

Compare and Contrast

Ideas in parts of this lesson explain comparisons and contrasts—they tell how things are alike and different. Active readers focus on comparisons and contrasts when they ask questions such as, How are measuring tools alike and different?

Make It Clear!

Scientists use tools to give them super-vision!
Some tools that do this include hand lenses
and microscopes.

Active Reading As you read these two
pages, circle words or phrases that signal
when things are alike and different.

Light microscopes let you see
tiny objects by using a light
source and lenses or mirrors
inside the microscope.

A magnifying box
has a lens in its lid.

A hand lens has one
lens with a handle.

Use forceps to pick up tiny objects
to view with magnifiers.

Use a dropper to move small
amounts of liquids for viewing.

Close, Closer, Closest!

Magnifying tools make objects look larger. Hold a hand lens close to one eye. Then move the hand lens closer to the object until it looks large and sharp. A magnifying box is like a hand lens in that it also has one lens. You can put things that are hard to hold, such as a bug, in it.

A **microscope** magnifies objects that are too tiny to be seen with the eye alone. Its power is much greater than that of a hand lens or magnifying box. Most microscopes have two or more lenses that work together.

▶ Draw a picture of how something you see might look if it was magnified.

Pond water as seen with just your eyes.

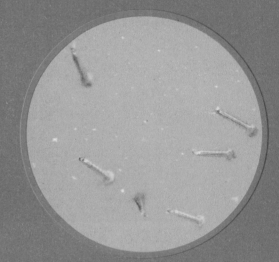

Pond water as seen through a hand lens.

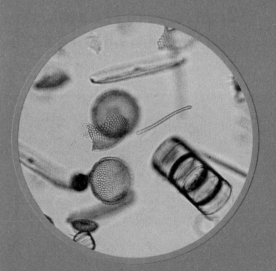

Pond water as seen through a microscope.

Measure It!

Measuring uses numbers to describe the world around you. There are several ways to measure and more than one tool or unit for each way.

Active Reading As you read the next page, circle the main idea.

A balance has a pan on either side. Put the object you want to measure on one pan and add masses to the other pan until they are balanced. The basic unit of mass is the gram.

The units on measuring tapes can be centimeters and meters or inches and feet.

ruler

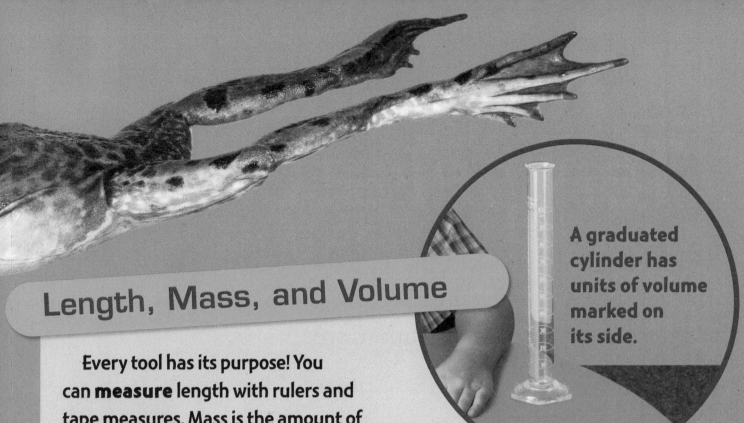

Length, Mass, and Volume

A graduated cylinder has units of volume marked on its side.

Every tool has its purpose! You can **measure** length with rulers and tape measures. Mass is the amount of matter in an object. It is measured with a pan balance. Volume is the amount of space a solid, liquid, or gas takes up.

The volume of a liquid can be measured with a **graduated cylinder** or a measuring cup or spoon. You can also use these tools to find the volume of solids that can be poured, such as sugar or salt. You **use numbers** to report measurements and **compare** objects. You can also **order** things using measurements. You can put pencils in order from shortest to longest.

Measuring cups and spoons are used because the amount of each ingredient is very important.

Do the Math!
Subtract Units

Use a metric ruler to measure the parts of the frog.

1. How many centimeters is the frog's longest front leg?

_____

2. How many centimeters is the frog's longest back leg?

_____

3. Now find the difference.

_____

4. Compare your measurements to those of other students.

_____

_____

Time and Temperature

How long did that earthquake shake? Which freezes faster, hot water or cold water? Scientists need tools to answer these questions!

Time

When you count the steady drip of a leaky faucet, you are thinking about time. You can **use time and space relationships.** Clocks and stopwatches are tools that measure time. The base unit of time is the second. One minute is equal to 60 seconds. One hour is equal to 60 minutes.

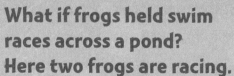

What if frogs held swim races across a pond? Here two frogs are racing.

START!

Temperature

When you say that ovens are hot or freezers are cold, you are thinking about **temperature**. A thermometer is the tool used to measure temperature. The base units of temperature are called degrees, but all degrees are not the same.

Scientists usually measure temperature in degrees Celsius. Most people around the world use Celsius, too. In the United States, however, degrees Fahrenheit are used to report the weather, body temperature, and in cooking.

▶ The first frog finished the race in 19 seconds. The second frog finished the race in 47 seconds. How much more quickly did the winning frog finish the race?

_____

_____

_____

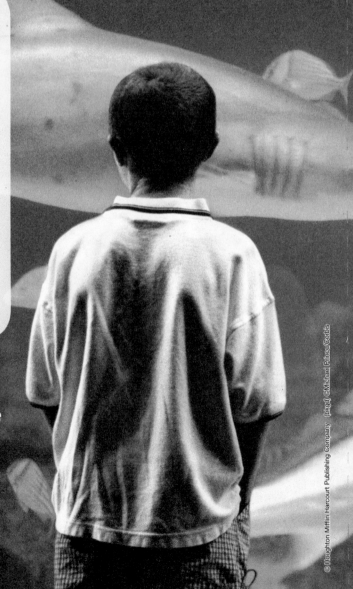

How Do You Care for Tropical Fish?

To care for tropical fish, you have to think like a scientist and use science tools.

Close Encounters

A public aquarium [uh•KWAIR•ee•uhm] is the place to see sharks and tropical fish. That's where many people get excited about keeping tropical fish at home. The word *aquarium* is used for both the big place you visit and the small tank in your home. Caring for both takes similar skills: observing, inferring, measuring, and recording data.

Does moving your aquarium in front of the window change the water's temperature?

What is the volume of water in your aquarium?

Keep Good Records

Keeping good records is important, whether you're recording data in your science notebook or making entries in your aquarium log. In your log, record the temperature every time you check it. Write the time you feed the fish and the volume of food you give them. Making correct measurements is part of being a good scientist.

Water test kits identify materials in the water.

Taking care of fish means checking the temperature.

Cause and Effect

Every change in an aquarium has a cause. Sometimes fish in an aquarium might become sick. Think of two things that might cause the fish to get sick.

_____

_____

_____

Sum It Up!

When you're done, use the answer key to
check and revise your work.

**The idea web below summarizes this lesson.
Complete the web.**

How Scientist Use Tools

1 They use hand lenses
and microscopes to make
things look

_____.

They use tools to measure.

2 Length is measured with

_____

_____.

3 A graduated
cylinder measures

_____.

4 Pan balances measure

_____.

5 They measure time
with clocks and

_____.

Answer Key: 1. bigger, 2. rulers and measuring tapes, 3. volume, 4. mass,
5. stopwatches

Name _____

Word Play

1 Write each term after its definition. Then find each term in the word search puzzle.

A. A tool used to measure mass _____

B. A temperature scale used by scientists _____

C. A tool used to pick up tiny objects _____

D. A tool used to measure volume _____

E. A tool you hold against your eye to make objects look bigger

   _____

F. How hot or cold something is _____

G. A tool that measures temperature _____

H. Something you measure with a stopwatch _____

I. How much space something take up _____

L	T	E	M	P	E	R	A	T	U	R	E	R	M	Y	O	L
U	H	R	P	A	M	I	L	C	E	L	S	I	U	S	V	W
K	E	E	A	V	S	U	N	B	O	W	L	M	A	X	Y	M
N	R	V	N	U	O	M	Z	O	O	L	I	S	S	T	F	O
G	M	C	B	E	U	L	I	H	T	M	A	Y	T	L	O	K
Y	O	Y	A	B	L	U	U	M	I	M	M	Y	O	R	R	J
F	M	S	L	K	K	Z	W	M	M	X	Q	I	P	Z	C	D
K	E	H	A	R	O	O	R	L	E	A	F	S	I	M	E	E
E	T	N	N	R	U	C	L	M	K	P	I	U	T	X	P	H
S	E	N	C	F	I	L	L	H	A	N	D	L	E	N	S	S
J	R	U	E	M	M	U	V	L	V	I	G	T	H	M	I	T
G	R	A	D	U	A	T	E	D	C	Y	L	I	N	D	E	R

Apply Concepts

In 2–5, tell which tool(s) you would use and how you would use them.

 thermometer

measuring spoons

 measuring tape

ruler

magnifying box

2 Find out how long your dog is from nose to tail.

_____

_____

_____

3 Decide if you need to wear a sweatshirt outdoors.

_____

_____

4 Make a bubble bath that has just the right amount of bubbles and is not too hot or too cold.

_____

_____

_____

_____

5 Examine a ladybug and count its legs without hurting it.

_____

_____

_____

_____

Take It Home!

Share what you have learned about measuring with your family. With a family member, identify examples of objects you could measure in or near your home.

28

Name _____

Essential Question

How Can You Measure Length?

Set a Purpose
What will you be able to do at the end of this investigation?

_____

_____

_____

Think About the Procedure
What will you think about when choosing the measurement tool for each item?

_____

_____

How will you choose the units that are best for each item?

_____

_____

Record Your Results
In the space below, make a table in which you record your measurements.

Draw Conclusions

1. How does choosing the best tool make measuring length easier?

_____

_____

_____

_____

_____

2. How do units affect the quality of a measurement?

_____

_____

_____

_____

_____

Analyze and Extend

1. Did groups who used the same tools as your group get the same results as you? Explain why or why not.

_____

_____

_____

_____

2. Why was it important to communicate your results with other groups? Explain.

_____

_____

_____

_____

3. When would someone want to use millimeters to find out who throws a ball the farthest? When would using millimeters not be a good choice? (1,000 mm = 1 m)

_____

_____

_____

_____

4. Think of another question you would like to ask about measuring.

_____

_____

_____

_____

Materials
Which tools should you use?

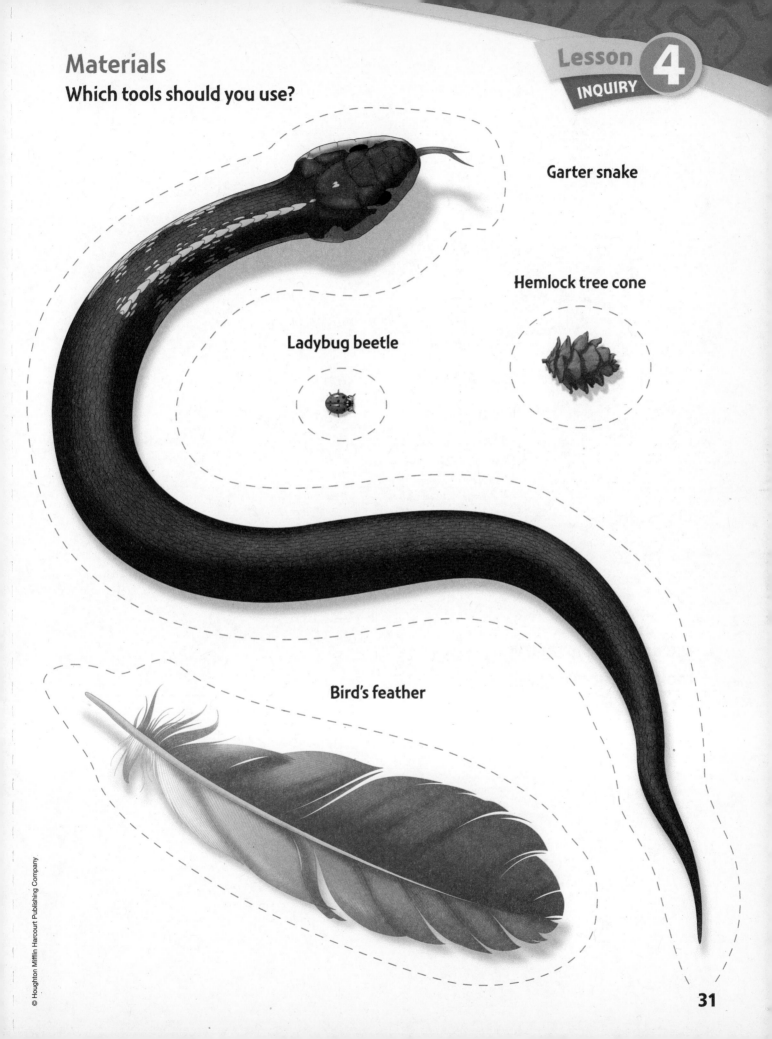

Garter snake

Hemlock tree cone

Ladybug beetle

Bird's feather

Essential Question

How Do Scientists Use Data?

🧠 Engage Your Brain!

People sometimes make statues out of blocks. If you could count how many blocks of each color there are, how would you record this information?

_____

_____

_____

_____

Active Reading

Lesson Vocabulary

List each term. As you learn about each one, make notes in the Interactive Glossary.

_____ _____

_____ _____

_____ _____

_____

Main Ideas

The main idea of a section is the most important idea. The main idea may be stated in the first sentence, or it may be stated elsewhere. Active readers look for main ideas by asking themselves, What is this section mostly about?

Show Me the Evidence

Scientists use observations to answer their questions. You can do this, too!

My data are my *evidence*. The data show that a raft with six planks floats twice as much weight as a raft with three planks.

Onisha, how do you know that a bigger raft can float more weight than a smaller one?

— I put the pennies on the raft with three planks. It held fewer pennies than the other raft.

Each science observation is a piece of **data.** For example, the number of pennies on a raft is data.

Onisha finished her investigation and thought about what it meant. She studied her data. Scientists use data as **evidence** to decide whether a hypothesis is or is not supported. Either way, scientists learn valuable things.

Scientists ask other scientists a lot of questions. They compare data. They repeat the investigation to see if they get the same results. Scientists review and talk about the evidence. They agree and disagree while respecting each other's ideas.

▶ Scientists might live too far away to meet face to face. What are three other ways they can share data and discuss evidence?

_____

_____

_____

_____

_____

_____

_____

_____

Communicating Data

Scientists record and display data so others can understand it. There are many ways and many tools to do this.

Active Reading As you read these two pages, circle a sentence that tells the main idea.

Models can help us understand things that are too big, small, or dangerous to do or observe.

▶ You want to find how high different kinds of balls bounce. You test each ball 20 times. How will you record and display your measurements?

_____

_____

After you **gather data**, you can share, or **communicate**, it with others in different ways. How can you **record data**? To show how birds get seeds from a feeder, you can use a camera. If you observe how a dog cares for her puppies, write in a journal.

Sometimes scientists use charts and graphs to help **interpret** and **display data**. A **chart** is a display that organizes data into rows and columns. A **data table** is a kind of chart for recording numbers. A **bar graph** is used to compare data about different events or groups. Bar graphs make it easier to see patterns or relationships in data.

These students made a bar graph and a data table to compare results.

Maps, like this world map, help to show the relationships between different objects or ideas.

▶ You want to show kinds of weather in different places. How could you display this information?

_____

_____

▶ You want to show the different layers that make up Earth's crust. What could you use?

_____

_____

How To Do It!

What are some ways to display data? You can use data tables, bar graphs, and line graphs. How can students use displays to show what they observed in the butterfly garden?

Active Reading As you read these two pages, draw boxes around two clue words that signal a sequence, or order.

DATA TABLE

Month	Number of Butterflies
March	5
April	5
May	9
June	14

BAR GRAPH

Butterfly Garden

How do you create a graph? First, look at the data table. Each column has a heading telling what information is in that column. Now, look at the graphs. Did you notice that the same headings are used to name the parts of the graphs?

On the graphs, look at the line next to the heading "Number of Butterflies." It looks like a number line, starting at zero and getting larger. It shows the number of butterflies.

To complete the bar graph, find the name of a month along the bottom. Then, move your finger up until you reach the number of butterflies for that month. Draw a bar to that point. To complete the line graph, draw points to show the number of butterflies for each month. Then, connect the points.

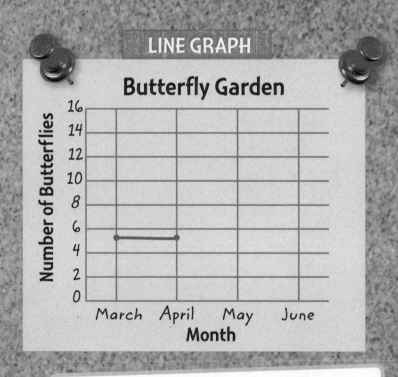

▶ Now it's your turn. Use the data table to help you complete the graphs for the months of May and June.

Why Graphs?

Sharing information with others is important to scientists. How do graphs help us share?

I can share these results with other scientists. They can repeat the experiment to see if they get different results.

Why did you use a graph instead of a data table?

A graph helps you see information quickly and recognize patterns.

DATA TABLE

Class	Number of Cans
Room 5	40
Room 8	55
Room 11	20
Room 12	35
Room 15	45

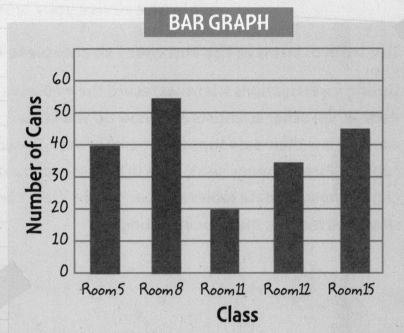

BAR GRAPH

Do the Math!
Interpret a Graph

Students collected evidence about a canned food drive in a data table. They organized the data in a graph.

1. Use the data table to find which class brought the least number of cans.

_____

2. Use the graph to find which class brought the greatest number of cans.

_____

3. Which was easier to use, the data table or the graph? Why?

_____

_____

_____

_____

_____

_____

_____

Sum It Up!

When you're done, use the answer key to check
and revise your work.

Use information in the summary to complete the graphic organizer.

During investigations scientists record their observations, or data. When other scientists ask, "How do you know?", they explain how their data supports their answers. Observations can be shared in many ways. Data in the form of numbers can be shown in data tables and bar graphs. Data can also be shared as models, maps, or in writing.

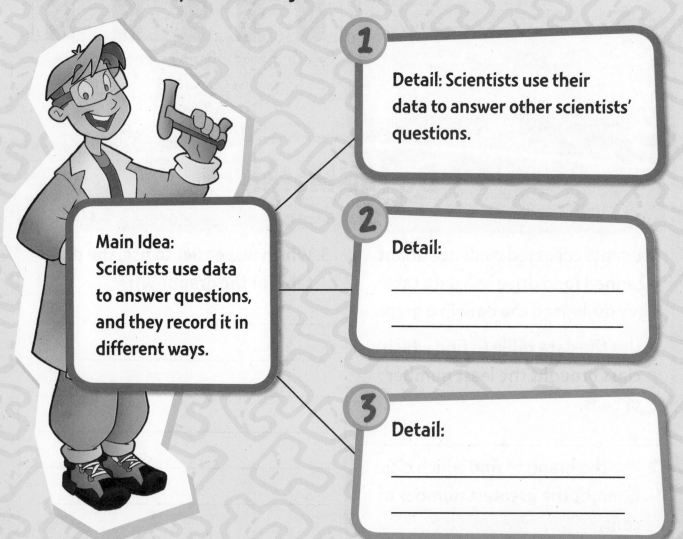

1 Detail: Scientists use their data to answer other scientists' questions.

Main Idea: Scientists use data to answer questions, and they record it in different ways.

2 Detail:
_____
_____

3 Detail:
_____
_____

Answer key: 2. Data can be shown in data tables and bar graphs. 3. Data can also be shared as models, maps, or in writing.

Word Play

Find the correct meaning and underline it.

1 Data
- tools used to measure
- steps in an investigation
- pieces of scientific information

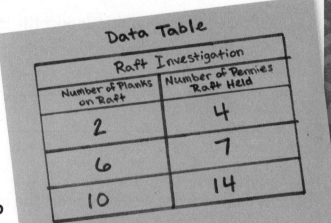

2 Evidence
- a kind of graph
- how much space something takes up
- the facts that show if a hypothesis is correct

3 Data table
- a chart for recording numbers
- the number of planks on a raft
- a piece of furniture used by scientists

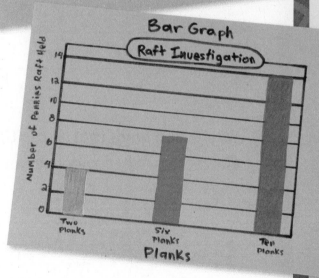

4 Bar graph
- a chart for recording numbers
- a graph in the shape of a circle
- a graph that shows how things compare

5 Communicate
- take a photograph
- share data with others
- collect and record data

Apply Concepts

Read the paragraph and answer questions 6–7.

One morning, your dad walks you and your sister to the school bus stop. When you get there, you wonder, "Has the bus come yet?"

6 What evidence would support the idea that the bus has not arrived yet?

_____

_____

7 What evidence would support the idea that the bus had already come?

_____

_____

_____

8 Your friend brags that he can throw a baseball 100 meters. What evidence would prove this?

_____

_____

_____

Take It Home! Share with your family what you have learned about recording evidence. With a family member, identify something you want to observe. Then decide how to record your data.

Name _____

Essential Question

How Do Your Results Compare?

Set a Purpose
What will you learn from this investigation?

_____

_____

State Your Hypothesis
Tell how you think the height of bubbles in water relates to the amount of dishwashing liquid used.

_____

_____

_____

Think About the Procedure
List the things you did that were the same each time.

_____

_____

_____

Describe the variable, the one thing you changed each time.

_____

_____

_____

Record Data
In the space below, make a table to record your measurements.

Draw Conclusions

Look back at your hypothesis. Did your results support it? Explain your answer.

_____

_____

_____

_____

Analyze and Extend

1. Why is it helpful to compare results with others?

_____

_____

_____

_____

2. What would you do if you found out that your results were very different from those of others?

_____

_____

_____

3. The bar graph below shows the height of the column of bubbles produced by equal amounts of three brands of dishwashing liquid. What does this data show?

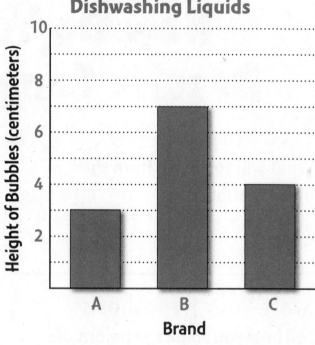

Bubbles Made by Dishwashing Liquids

_____

_____

_____

_____

4. Think of other questions you would like to ask about bubbles.

_____

_____

_____

_____

1
A meteorologist is a person who studies weather.

2
Meteorologists use tools to measure temperature, wind speed, and air pressure.

3
Meteorologists use data they collect to forecast the weather.

6
THINGS
You Should
Know About
Meteorologists

4
Computers help meteorologists share weather data from around the world.

5
Keeping good records helps meteorologists see weather patterns.

6
Meteorologists' forecasts help people stay safe during bad weather.

Be a Meteorologist

Answer the questions below using the Weather Forecast bar graph.

1. What was the temperature on Thursday? _____

2. Which day was cloudy and rainy? _____

3. How much cooler was it on Tuesday than Thursday? _____

4. Which day was partly cloudy? _____

5. Compare the temperatures on Tuesday and Friday. Which day had the higher temperature? _____

6. In the forecast below, which day has the highest temperature _____? The lowest? _____

WEATHER FORECAST

Temperature °F

90
85
80
75
70

Monday Tuesday Wednesday Thursday Friday

Day of week

Unit 1 Review

Name _____

Vocabulary Review

Use the terms in the box to complete the sentences.

> bar graph
> evidence
> experiment
> hypothesis
> variable

1. You can share the results of an investigation with others by using a(n) _____.

2. An observation often leads to a testable question known as a(n) _____.

3. A planned study meant to answer a question is called a(n) _____.

4. It is very important to test only one _____, or thing that changes, at a time.

5. A hypothesis should be supported by the _____.

Science Concepts

Fill in the letter of the choice that best answers the question.

6. Alix wants to conduct an experiment to find out how fertilizer affects bean plants. Which of the following is a hypothesis that she could test?

   (A) Alix will need bean seeds, soil, fertilizer, and water.

   (B) All the plants must get the same amount of sunlight.

   (C) Fertilizer can be organic or chemical.

   (D) Fertilizer causes bean plants to grow larger and faster.

7. Samuel noticed that small dogs often have a high-pitched bark, while big dogs often have a low-pitched bark. Would a scientist consider this an experiment?

   (A) Yes, because you could study many different sizes and types of dogs to find out if it is true.

   (B) Yes, because there may be a scientific reason for the difference in dog barks.

   (C) No, because this is an observation, not an experiment.

   (D) No, because it is illegal to use experiments to learn about animals.

Science Concepts

Fill in the letter of the choice that best answers the question.

8. Zelia performed an experiment to see if a toy car would travel down a ramp faster on wax paper or sandpaper. For each type of surface, she timed how long it took for the same toy car to reach the bottom of the ramp. Her results are shown in the table.

	Wax paper	Sandpaper
Trial 1	8 seconds	12 seconds
Trial 2	7 seconds	11 seconds
Trial 3	8 seconds	23 seconds
Trial 4	9 seconds	13 seconds

Which trial has most likely been recorded incorrectly?

Ⓐ Trial 1

Ⓑ Trial 2

Ⓒ Trial 3

Ⓓ Trial 4

9. A tool often used in science is shown below.

For which task would this tool most likely be used?

Ⓐ observing bread mold closely

Ⓑ observing the color of a leaf

Ⓒ observing planets in the solar system

Ⓓ observing the texture of a rock

10. Gabe is interested in animals that live in the desert. He wants to learn more about what desert animals eat. Which of these should Gabe use in his investigation?

Ⓐ a model of a desert animal

Ⓑ a chart showing monthly rainfall in the desert

Ⓒ a data table showing food for desert animals

Ⓓ a graph of average temperatures in the desert

11. The picture below shows a tool used for measuring liquids.

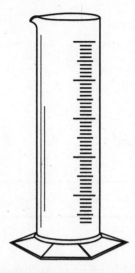

Which could this tool measure?

Ⓐ mass

Ⓑ length

Ⓒ temperature

Ⓓ volume

12. Ranjit wants to build shelves in a closet. The closet is 2 meters wide. The wooden boards he wants to use are more than 2 meters long. He will need to measure the boards, then use a saw to cut the correct length. What tool should Ranjit use to measure the correct length of the boards?

Ⓐ a balance

Ⓑ a pedometer

Ⓒ a tape measure

Ⓓ a graduated cylinder

13. Martina is investigating how different types of soil affect radish seed germination. She plans to plant the same number of radish seeds in three different types of soil. Each day for a week, she will count the number of radish seeds that emerge from the soil. What should Martina use to collect and organize her information?

Ⓐ a model

Ⓑ a data table

Ⓒ a stopwatch

Ⓓ a thermometer

14. Zane is doing an experiment in which he measures the temperature of the water in three different tanks. Which of the following tools would he use?

Ⓐ a thermometer

Ⓑ a pan balance

Ⓒ a microscope

Ⓓ a stopwatch

Apply Inquiry and Review the Big Idea

Write the answers to these questions.

15. This picture shows a model of the sun, Earth, and Earth's moon.

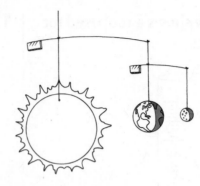

What is the advantage of using a model like the one shown?

_____

_____

16. Luisa was studying whether certain tropical flowers would bloom even when temperatures dropped below 15 degrees Celsius. She placed the blooming plants outside. She measured the temperature outside each day for seven days. She observed that the plants bloomed each day of the week. The graph shows the data she collected.

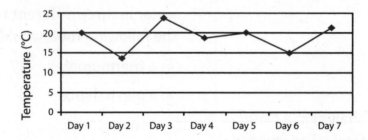

What is one conclusion Luisa could draw based on the data in her graph?

_____

_____

17. Two teams measured the mass and the volume of the same rubber duck. One team found the mass to be 65 g and the volume to be 150 mL. The other team found that the mass was 63 g and the volume was 149 mL. What could explain these differences?

_____

_____

The Engineering Process

Big Idea

Technology is all around us. The design process is used to develop new types of technology to meet people's needs.

Union Station in Indianapolis, Indiana

I Wonder Why

This building was built in 1853. How has the building process changed since then? Stayed the same? *Turn the page to find out.*

Here's why In 1853, tools were less complex than they are today, and they were not electric. But today's builders still have to draw plans, choose materials, and make sure the building is safe to use.

In this unit, you will explore the Big Idea, the Essential Questions, and the Investigations on the Inquiry Flipchart.

Levels of Inquiry Key ■ DIRECTED ■ GUIDED ■ INDEPENDENT

Track Your Progress

Big Idea Technology is all around us. The design process is used to develop new types of technology to meet people's needs.

Essential Questions

Now I Get the Big Idea!

Science Notebook

Before you begin each lesson, be sure to write your thoughts about the Essential Question.

Essential Question

How Do Engineers Use the Design Process?

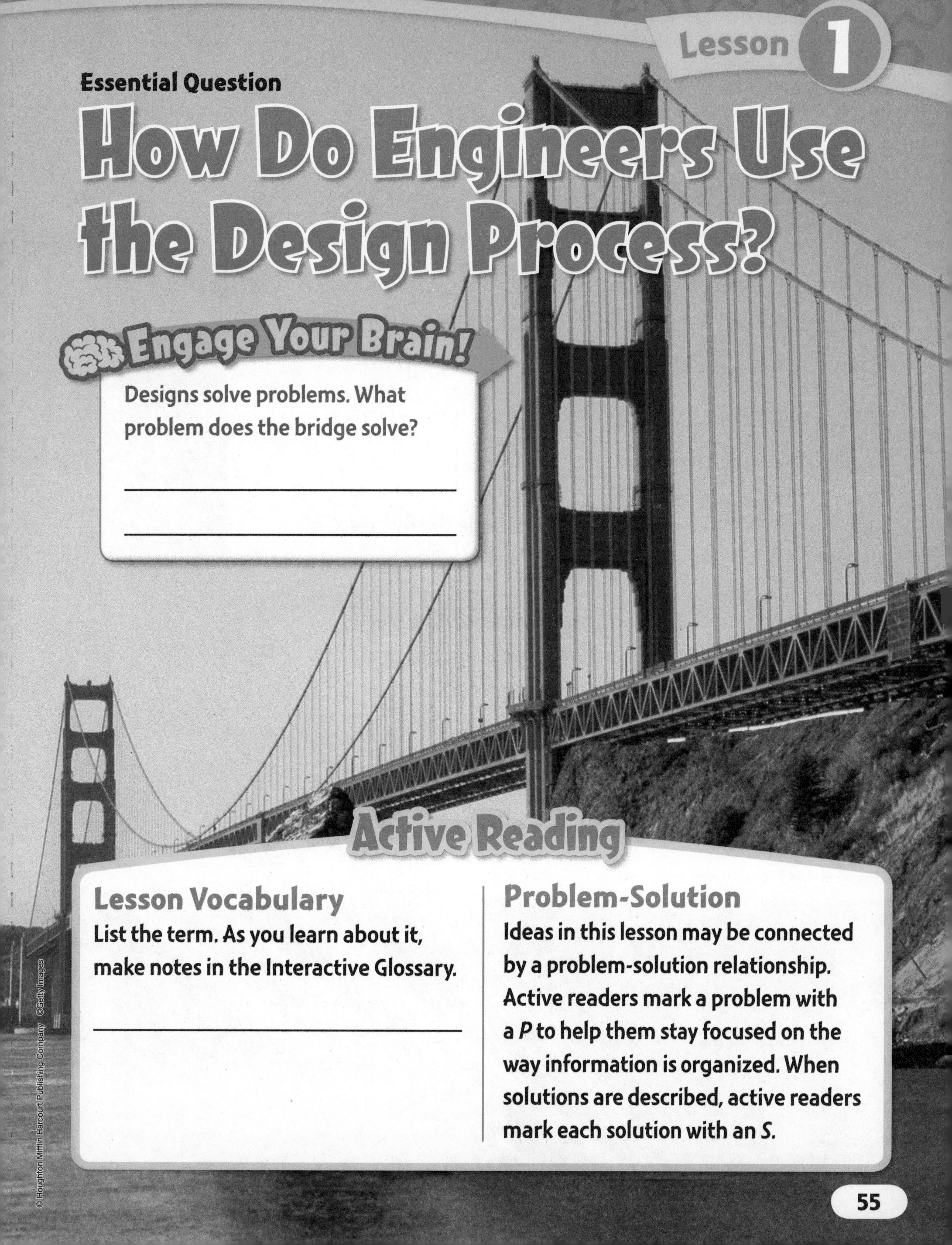

Engage Your Brain!

Designs solve problems. What problem does the bridge solve?

_____

_____

Active Reading

Lesson Vocabulary

List the term. As you learn about it, make notes in the Interactive Glossary.

_____

Problem-Solution

Ideas in this lesson may be connected by a problem-solution relationship. Active readers mark a problem with a *P* to help them stay focused on the way information is organized. When solutions are described, active readers mark each solution with an *S*.

The Design Process

To get to school, you may have ridden your bike or taken the bus. These are two different ways of getting to school, but they have something in common.

Active Reading As you read this page, circle the five steps of the design process and number each step.

Both of the methods of transportation above were developed by someone who used the design process. The **design process** is the process engineers follow to solve problems. It is a multistep process that includes finding a problem, planning and building, testing and improving, redesigning, and communicating results.

The William H. Natcher Bridge makes crossing the Ohio River easy and fast!

An engineer used the design process to design the supports for this bridge.

The design process can help people solve problems or design creative solutions. Look at the picture of the Ohio River between Rockport, Indiana, and Owensboro, Kentucky. In the past, only one bridge connected these cities. Over time, the bridge got very crowded. In this lesson, you'll see how the design process was used to design a solution to this problem.

How Do Inventions Help You?

Think of an invention that has made your life easier. What problem did it solve? How do you think the inventor used the design process to find the solution?

_____

_____

_____

_____

_____

Finding a Problem

The design process starts with finding a problem. An engineer can't design a solution without first knowing what the problem is!

Active Reading As you read these two pages, put brackets [ ] around sentences that describe the problem, and write *P* in front of the brackets. Put brackets around sentences that describe the steps toward a solution, and write *S* in front of the brackets.

A team of scientists and engineers worked together. They saw there was a lot of traffic on the old bridge. People of both cities needed another way to cross the Ohio River. The team studied the best way to get the most people and cars across the river.

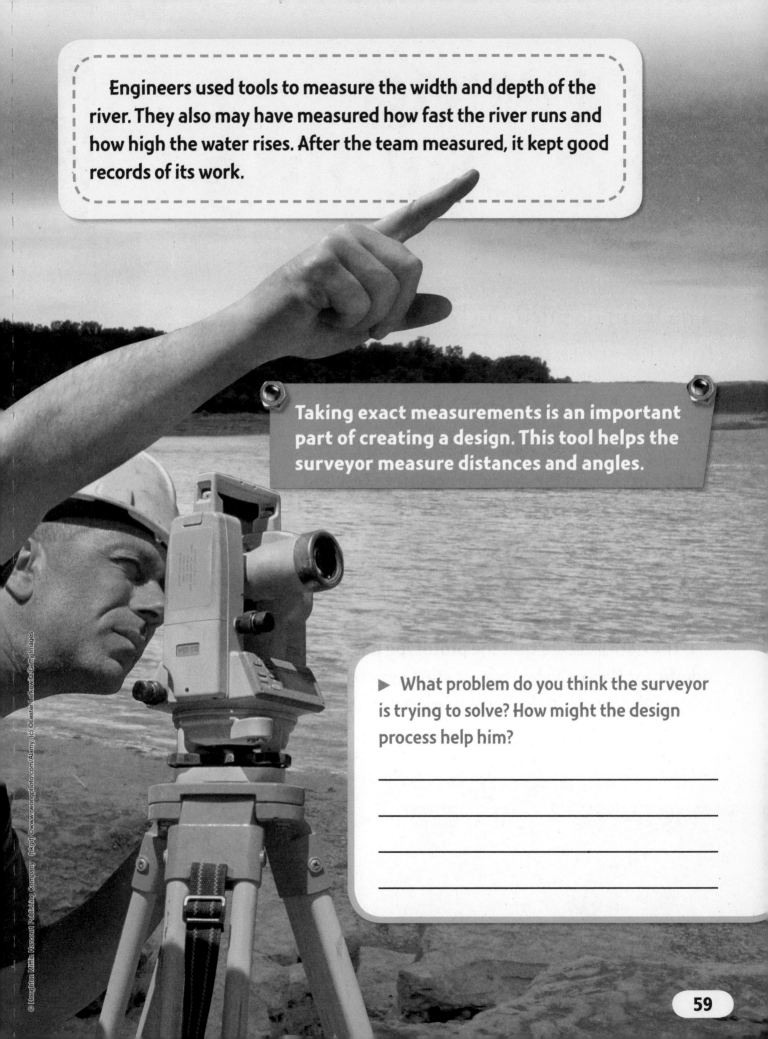

Engineers used tools to measure the width and depth of the river. They also may have measured how fast the river runs and how high the water rises. After the team measured, it kept good records of its work.

Taking exact measurements is an important part of creating a design. This tool helps the surveyor measure distances and angles.

▶ What problem do you think the surveyor is trying to solve? How might the design process help him?

_____

_____

_____

_____

Planning and Building

The team decided the best solution would be to build another bridge across the Ohio River.

 **Active Reading** As you read these two pages, underline the sentences that describe steps in the design process.

The next step in the design process is to test and improve the prototype. The engineers gather data about important features of the bridge design, such as how stable it is and how much weight it can support. The team may modify minor aspects of the design based on this data.

If the data indicate that the prototype has significant flaws, the team must start over again. They redesign the bridge by making major changes to their initial plan.

Engineers carefully evaluated and tested the safety of the William H. Natcher Bridge. They made sure that builders followed the plans and used the correct materials.

The last step in the design process is to communicate the solution. Bridge inspectors used their findings, or evidence, to write reports. They used mathematical representations, such as graphs, tables, and drawings, to explain that the bridge was safe to open. Engineers could now use this information to make improvements and build bridges in other places!

The prototype helped builders know how wide, tall, and long to make the bridge.

Communication Is Key!

List three other ways you might communicate the results of a project to others.

_____

_____

How Do Designs Get Better Over Time?

An engineer's work is never done! Every invention can be improved. For example, instead of building a fire in a wood stove or turning on a gas or electric oven, you can use a microwave to cook your food.

Just as with stoves, engineers have come up with newer and better designs for cell phones. Forty years ago, cell phones were bulky and heavy. Today, the smallest cell phone is not much bigger than a watch!

Martin Cooper invented the first cell phone in 1973. It was 13 inches long, weighed about 2 pounds, and allowed only 30 minutes of talk time.

▶ What might happen if cell phones get too small?

_____

_____

_____

Cell phones today do much more than just make phone calls. They let you take pictures, look up directions, listen to music, watch TV, or search the Internet.

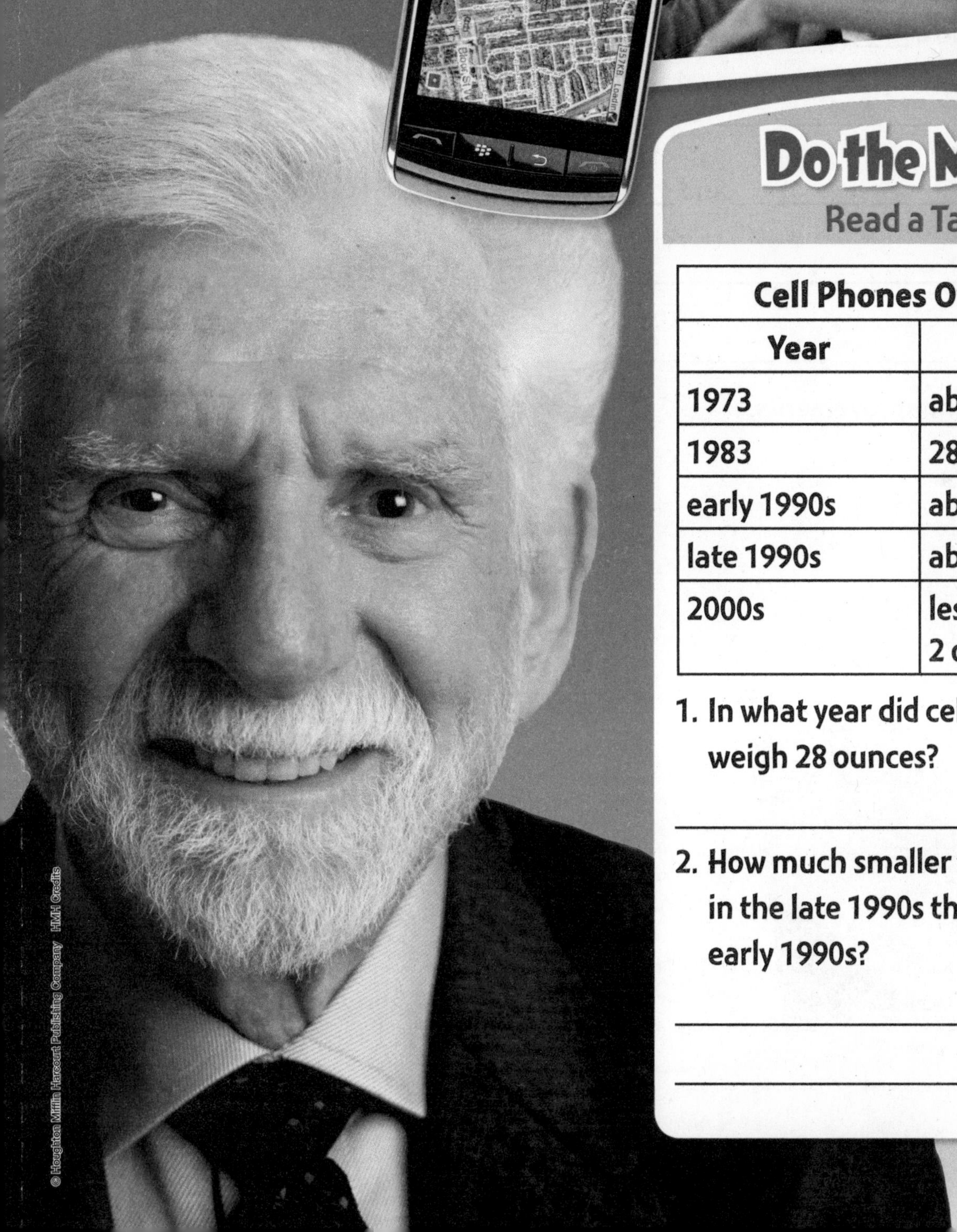

Do the Math!
Read a Table

Cell Phones Over Time	
Year	**Weight**
1973	about 2 pounds
1983	28 ounces
early 1990s	about 8 ounces
late 1990s	about 4 ounces
2000s	less than 2 ounces

1. In what year did cell phones weigh 28 ounces?

_____

2. How much smaller were phones in the late 1990s than in the early 1990s?

_____

_____

Sum It Up!

When you're done, use the answer key to check and revise your work.

Complete the step of the design process in each sentence.

1

1. First, find a _____.

2. Second, _____ and _____ a prototype.

3. Third, _____ and _____ the prototype.

4. Fourth, _____ the prototype as necessary.

5. Fifth, _____ the solution, test data, and your improvements.

Answer Key: 1. problem 2. plan, build 3. test, improve 4. redesign 5. communicate

 **Brain Check**

Name _____

Word Play

1 Use these words to complete the puzzle.

Across

2. A plan for a solution that may use many drawings

6. A way of letting people know about a design

Down

1. Something that needs a solution

3. The steps engineers follow to solve problems

4. To judge how well a design works

5. The outcome of the design process

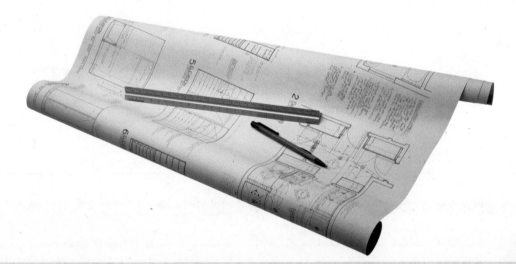

| problem | process | solution | design | evaluate | communicate |

2 Kyle's pet hamster is curious! It always finds a way out of its cage. Use the design process to help Kyle solve this problem.

_____

_____

_____

_____

_____

3 Label each of the following as a problem or a solution.

_____ _____ _____ _____

Take It Home!

Share what you have learned about the design process with your family. With a family member, identify products that are good examples of the design process. What problems do they solve?

Name _____

How Can You Design a Tree House?

Set a Purpose
What will you do in this activity?

_____

_____

_____

_____

State Your Hypothesis
What parts of the design process will you use in this activity?

_____

_____

_____

_____

Think About the Procedure
Why is it important to have a plan before you start building the tree house?

_____

_____

_____

_____

_____

_____

What problems do you identify? How might you solve these problems?

_____

_____

_____

_____

_____

_____

Record Your Data

In the space below, draw a prototype for your plan.

[blank box for drawing]

Draw Conclusions

Why do you think it is important to build a prototype for your plan before you start building the actual tree house?

_____

_____

_____

Analyze and Extend

1. Suppose you were going to use the design process to build the tree house you've designed. What more would you need to do before you began building?

_____

_____

_____

2. As you look at your prototype and think about it, is there any part you would want to redesign? Why?

_____

_____

_____

_____

_____

_____

_____

_____

3. What other things would you like to know about how the design process is used to plan projects like your tree house?

_____

_____

_____

_____

_____

_____

_____

68

Essential Question

How Are Technology and Society Related?

Engage Your Brain!

Find the answer to the following question in this lesson and record it here.

Where is the technology in this picture?

_____

_____

_____

_____

Active Reading

Lesson Vocabulary

Write the term. As you learn about it, make notes in the Interactive Glossary.

_____

Signal Words: Details

Signal words show connections between ideas. *For example* signals examples of an idea. *Also* signals added facts. Active readers remember what they read because they are alert to signal words that identify examples and facts about a topic.

Technology

What is technology? Look at this train station. Nearly everything you see is an example of technology.

Active Reading As you read these two pages, circle two clue words or phrases that signal a detail such as an example or an added fact.

Technology is anything that people make or do that changes the natural world. Technology meets people's wants or needs. Technology is not just computers and cell phones. Think about the things in a train station. They all have a purpose. The technology in a train station helps people travel easily. Can you imagine how different the world would be without technology?

Suitcase

A suitcase contains a traveler's needs. For example, it can carry clothing, shoes, pajamas, a hairbrush, a toothbrush, and toothpaste. All of these items are examples of technology.

Train Schedule Board

A schedule board tells when trains depart. It also names the track each train leaves on. This technology allows train schedules to be updated quickly as needed.

Clock

Clocks are also technology. They tell travelers what time it is. Travelers can tell how long it will be before their train arrives. They can also find out if they are late for their train.

INFORMATION HARLEM LINE DEPA

ATTENTION CUSTOMERS:
NEVER LEAVE PACKAGES UNATTENDED
UNATTENDED ITEMS MAY BE REMOVED
BY THE MTA POLICE DEPARTMENT.
THANK YOU FOR YOUR COOPERATION!

TIME TRK DESTINATION REMARKS
4:15 106 NO. WH PLAINS FORDHAM — 19
4:48 17 SOUTHEAST WHITE PLAIN
5:22 32 HARSIC WHITE PLAIN
5:25 105 NO. WH PLAINS MELROSE — 19
5:48 17 SOUTHEAST WHITE PLAIN

What Do Technologies Do?

List two technologies that you see in the photo. Tell what each does.

_____

_____

_____

Technology Through Time

A train today is different from a train from 100 years ago or even 50 years ago!

Steam locomotive 1800s

Steam locomotives were developed in the early 1800s. They were powered by burning wood or coal that heated water to make steam.

Active Reading As you read these two pages, draw two lines under the main idea.

Technology is always changing. The earliest trains were dragged along grooves in the ground. Today, superfast trains can travel hundreds of miles an hour. Train tracks have changed over time, too. New technology made tracks of iron. These could carry heavier loads. Trains could be larger and also travel faster. These improvements made trains more useful to people. Improvements in technology make trains work better, faster, and more easily.

Modern switches operate electronically. Computers send a signal that changes the tracks that the train will follow.

The earliest track switches were moved by hand.

Diesel engine 1900s

By the mid-1900s, the diesel engine had replaced the steam locomotive. Diesel is a type of fuel.

Maglev train 2000s

The fastest trains don't run on tracks anymore. Maglev trains ride on powerful magnets.

Do the Math!
Interpret a Table

Look at the table. How much faster is the Maglev train than the steam locomotive at maximum speed?

Train Speeds	
Train	Maximum speed (mph)
Steam locomotive	126
Diesel engine	100
Bullet Train	275
Maglev	361

_____

_____

_____

Technology and Society

Technology and society are connected. Technology affects how people live and what they do. People also affect technology by inventing new things.

Active Reading As you read these two pages, put brackets [ ] around the sentence that describes a problem and write *P* next to it. Underline the sentence that describes the solution and write *S* next to it.

Trains are an example of technology's connection to society. Trains carry people and cargo long distances. Resources, such as coal, can be carried long distances in a few days. Before trains, people in California may not have been able to get coal easily. People affect new train technology by finding ways for trains to cross high bridges or to tunnel through mountains. New technology helps trains meet people's needs and wants.

Some cities are far away from where coal is found and steel is produced. Train technology helps resources reach people in faraway cities.

Although trains through the Swiss Alps are safer than trucks on a road, only small trains can pass. The cars, roads, trains, and tracks are all transportation technologies that help people and goods move around the globe.

This new tunnel is beneath the Swiss Alps. The machine behind the workers is a technology that was used to help drill the tunnel. Large trains will be able to use the tunnel. Now people will be able to save more time traveling between cities.

Trains of the Future?

How would you change trains in the future? How would your changes affect society?

_____

_____

_____

_____

_____

Freight trains have refrigerator cars for keeping food fresh. This technology means that food can then be carried safely over long distances.

How Does Technology Affect You?

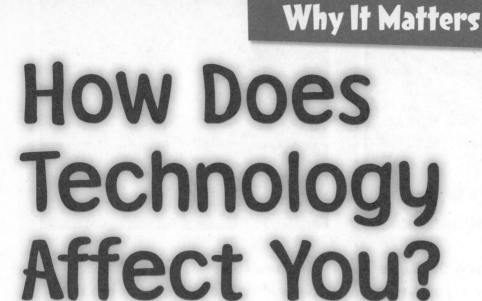

Technologies are always changing. Cars replaced horse-drawn carriages, and maybe someday flying cars will replace the cars we drive today!

Active Reading As you read this page, draw boxes around the names of the things that are being compared.

Think about the technology you use at school and at home. Have you noticed how they have changed? New televisions look different from older ones. Newer computers look much different, too. These newer technologies also do more than their older versions. Technology keeps improving with the goal of making life better.

Cell phone

Do you think when your grandparents were children they had the technology this boy has today?

Technology Changes

This camera uses film, which can store only about 20 images on a roll.

Digital cameras store hundreds of images. Images can be deleted for more space.

Cars in the 1960s used a lot of oil and gas and caused air pollution.

Hybrid cars use both electricity and gas to operate. They cause less air pollution.

Then and Now

Look at the technology below. What can you do with this technology today that people couldn't do 50 years ago?

Earlier telephones had rotary dials and were connected to the wall.

_____

_____

You could not easily edit your work on this typewriter.

_____

_____

Sum It Up!

When you're done, use the answer key to check and revise your work.

Complete the summary. Use the information to complete the graphic organizer.

Summarize

Technology is all around you. It can be very simple, like (1) _____.
At a train station, you may see a (2) _____ or a (3) _____.
If you live in a city you may see (4) _____ and (5) _____.
Even in your classroom at school you have a (6) _____, and you may even have a (7) _____.

Main Idea: Technology can be as simple as a fence or as complex as a space station.

(8) Detail: Technology can be complex	(9) Detail: Technology can be simple	Detail: Technology can be simple, like a fence.
_____	_____	
_____	_____	
_____	_____	
_____	_____	

Answer key: Sample answers: 1. shoes **2.** bench **3.** clock **4.** cars **5.** trains **6.** pencil **7.** computer **8.** like a car **9.** like a pencil

Brain Check

Name _____

Word Play

1 Write four words from the box that are examples of technology.

fence	giraffe	cell phone	rock
horse	car	leaf	stove

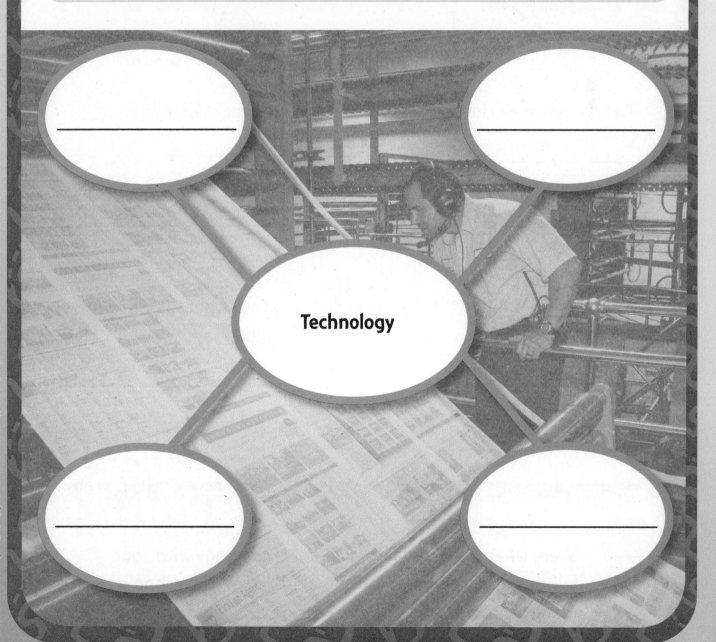

Technology

Apply Concepts

In 2–5, tell which technology you would use and how you would use it.

cell phone

magnifying glass

train

ruler

garden shovel

2 Get the lunch you left at home

_____
_____
_____

4 Plant vegetables in your garden

_____
_____
_____

3 Visit a friend in another state

_____
_____
_____

5 Find out what the fine print on a coupon says

_____
_____
_____

Take It Home!

Share what you have learned about technology with your family. With a family member, make a list of the technology in the kitchen of your home.

Name _____

Essential Question

How Can We Improve a Design?

Set a Purpose
What will you discover in this activity?

_____

_____

Think About the Procedure
How could you and your partner redesign the bridge to make it stronger?

_____

_____

_____

_____

Do you and your partner have different ideas for changing the bridge? Explain.

_____

_____

_____

_____

Record Your Data
Sketch your idea for a new bridge design. Make notes about how it differs from the first bridge.

Draw Conclusions

What were the best features of your design? What were the worst features? Explain.

_____

_____

_____

_____

_____

Analyze and Extend

1. Look at the bridges that other students made. What did all the new bridges that worked have in common?

_____

_____

_____

_____

2. What were the main reasons that the first bridge collapsed?

_____

_____

_____

_____

_____

3. How could looking at the design of other bridges help you redesign your own bridge?

_____

_____

_____

_____

_____

4. What other questions do you have about how things can be redesigned?

_____

_____

_____

_____

8 Things YOU SHOULD KNOW ABOUT Civil Engineers

DETOUR

1 Civil engineers plan the structures that are built in cities and towns. Roads and bridges are some of the things they plan.

2 The projects that civil engineers build need to be safe. They must hold up to daily use.

3 Civil engineers improve how we live. They help people get the things they need.

4 Civil engineers are important to a growing city or town. They look at the need for new structures.

5 Civil engineers keep cars and trucks moving. They fix roads that are no longer safe.

6 Civil engineers make drawings called construction plans.

7 Civil engineers use tools, such as compasses and rulers. Many engineers use computers.

8 Some civil engineers measure the surface of the land. They use this data to plan buildings.

Engineering Emergency!

Match the problems that can be solved by a civil engineer with its solution in the illustration. Write the number of the problem in the correct triangle on the picture.

1 We have an energy shortage! We can harness the river's energy to generate electricity.

2 The city is getting crowded! More people are moving here. They need more places to live and work.

3 The streets are always jammed. We have a transportation crisis!

4 The nearest bridge is too far away. We need a faster and easier way to get across the river.

Think About It!

If you were a civil engineer, what kind of changes would you make where you live?

_____

_____

Name _____

Vocabulary Review

Use the terms in the box to complete the sentences.

> design process
> technology

1. When Ms. Simm's third graders designed a tunnel, they followed steps in a _____.

2. A dishwasher is an example of something that makes a family's life easier and is a kind of _____.

Science Concepts

Fill in the letter of the choice that best answers the question.

3. The Johnson family decided to purchase a new vehicle. An important feature they searched for is four-wheel drive, because four-wheel drive works well in snow. Why is the invention of four-wheel drive a kind of technology?

   Ⓐ It solves the problem of increasing vehicle size.

   Ⓑ It meets the needs of drivers.

   Ⓒ It protects the environment.

   Ⓓ It decreases safety.

4. Stewart will be working with a team to design an improved outdoor light. What should they do before beginning improvements?

   Ⓐ improve their new design

   Ⓑ keep the old design just as it is

   Ⓒ test their new design

   Ⓓ test the old design

5. What is the **main** goal of the design process?

   Ⓐ to find solutions to problems

   Ⓑ to give scientists something to do

   Ⓒ to make charts and graphs

   Ⓓ to write articles for magazines

6. Grace, Miguel, and Amelia are studying how improving technologies can affect the environment. They have to design an invention that affects the environment in a positive way. Which invention do you think they picked?

   Ⓐ a bus that uses more gas than others

   Ⓑ a car tire that cannot be recycled

   Ⓒ an electric train that does not run on fuel

   Ⓓ a new fabric made from rare plants

Science Concepts

Fill in the letter of the choice that best answers the question.

7. Grocery stores can be very busy places. After people fill up their carts with what they need, they may have to stand in line for a while. The inventor of self-checkout lanes improved technology to help consumers. What new needs could self-checkout lanes cause?

Ⓐ colder freezer and refrigerator sections

Ⓑ automatic-bagging technology

Ⓒ safer pesticide use on produce

Ⓓ improved travel technology

8. Kelsey is researching new computers. She wants to find the computer with the newest technology. Which computer is she most likely to choose?

Ⓐ the biggest computer

Ⓑ the least expensive computer

Ⓒ the oldest computer

Ⓓ the computer with the fastest processing speed

9. What problem did adding air conditioning to cars solve?

Ⓐ Car engines got too hot during the summer.

Ⓑ People got too cold inside cars during the winter.

Ⓒ People got too hot inside cars during the summer.

Ⓓ The car radio got too hot during the hot summer days.

10. This is a technology that helped John's grandmother.

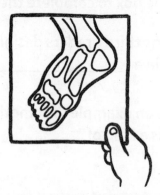

How did this technology most likely help John's grandmother?

Ⓐ It showed his grandmother that she was wearing the wrong size shoe.

Ⓑ It showed his grandmother what type of socks she should wear.

Ⓒ It showed that his grandmother's foot did not have bones.

Ⓓ It showed his grandmother's broken bones.

11. Scientists notice a problem with an engine. It is getting too hot after it runs for a long time. What should the scientists do **next**?

Ⓐ take the engine apart

Ⓑ plan and build a new engine

Ⓒ test and improve the new engine design

Ⓓ communicate results of the new engine design

12. An engineer designs a new engine, but one of the parts keeps melting. The engine can get hotter than 240 °C. Look at the table.

Material	Melting Point (°C)
potassium	64
plastic	120
tin	232
aluminum	660

Which material would you suggest the engineer use in the next design?

Ⓐ aluminum

Ⓑ plastic

Ⓒ potassium

Ⓓ tin

13. Suppose you are digging a stone out of the ground with a shovel. You have a problem after you dig all the dirt around the stone. The stone is too heavy to lift. What is your **best** option in solving this problem?

Ⓐ continue to try lifting it yourself

Ⓑ start over and pick a smaller rock

Ⓒ use a bigger shovel

Ⓓ use a tractor to pull it out of the ground

14. Suppose you are in a tree house you built. You notice that one of the boards is broken and could cause an accident. How could you improve your design?

Ⓐ paint the board with a bright color

Ⓑ replace the board with stronger wood

Ⓒ replace the entire floor

Ⓓ tear down the tree house

15. The chart below shows the number of miles per gallon of gas used by some cars. The cars that use the least gas travel more miles per gallon. How many cars use the least amount of gas?

Gas Mileage Per Gallon of Gasoline

Miles Per Gallon	Tally of Car Models
9–12	I
13–16	III
17–20	IIII
21–25	III
26–30	IIIII II
31–34	IIIII IIII
35–40	II

Each tally mark represents 1 model car.

Ⓐ 1

Ⓑ 2

Ⓒ 7

Ⓓ 9

Apply Inquiry and Review the Big Idea

Write the answers to these questions.

Use the picture to answer question 16.

16. Write three kinds of technology shown in the scene and describe how each improves society.

_____

_____

_____

17. You move to a new home with a doghouse in the backyard. Your small dog cannot get into the doghouse easily because it is raised up off the ground.

What is the problem? What can you do to solve this problem?

_____

_____

_____

Plants and Animals

Big Idea

All living things go through a cycle of growth. Living things have adaptations that help them survive in their environments.

mantis shrimp

I Wonder Why

Why is this mantis shrimp these colors? *Turn the page to find out.*

Here's why The colorful shell of the mantis shrimp helps it blend in with its surroundings. Blending in helps the mantis shrimp hide from predators and surprise prey.

In this unit, you will explore the Big Idea, the Essential Questions, and the Investigations on the Inquiry Flipchart.

Levels of Inquiry Key ■ DIRECTED ■ GUIDED ■ INDEPENDENT

Track Your Progress

Big Idea All living things go through a cycle of growth. Living things have adaptations that help them survive in their environments.

Essential Questions

Now I Get the Big Idea!

Science Notebook

Before you begin each lesson, be sure to write your thoughts about the Essential Question.

Essential Question

What Are Some Plant Life Cycles?

Engage Your Brain!

Find the answer to the following question in this lesson and record it here.

How is this hummingbird part of the plant's life cycle?

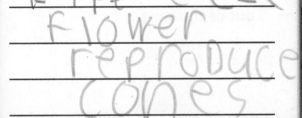

Life cycle
Flower
reproduce
cones

Active Reading

Lesson Vocabulary

List the terms. As you learn about each one, make notes in the Interactive Glossary.

germin   reproduce

Compare and Contrast

Many ideas in this lesson are connected because they explain comparisons and contrasts—how things are alike and different. Active readers stay focused on comparisons and contrasts when they ask themselves, How are these things alike? How are they different?

The Cycle of a Plant's Life

Most plants come from seeds, but how? And where do seeds come from? It's all part of the life cycle of a plant.

Active Reading As you read these two pages, find and underline the definitions of *life cycle, germinate, flower, reproduce,* and *cone.*

Plants go through many stages in their lives. These stages form a *cycle,* or pattern, that repeats again and again. The stages an *organism,* or living thing, goes through during its life is its **life cycle**.

Most plants come from seeds. A seed **germinates** when it breaks open and a small plant grows out of it. The plant grows into an adult, which forms flowers in some types of plants. A **flower** is the part of some plants that enables them to **reproduce**, or make more plants similar to themselves.

Flowers can be colorful, dull, big, or small! Flowers have male parts and female parts that are involved in reproduction.

Seedling

When a seed is watered, it begins to germinate. A *seedling* is the tiny new plant that comes out of the seed.

Seed

Inside each seed is a plant in an early stage of its development. The hard outer covering of the seed protects it. These seeds will grow into large tomato plants.

Adult Plant

The seedling grows into an adult plant. The adult tomato plant makes flowers. In flowering plants, seeds are produced in the flowers.

▶ Circle one step in the cycle. Why does the cycle stop if that step is removed?

_____

_____

_____

Fruit

The flowers fall off the plant, and the plant makes fruit. The fruit holds the seeds.

Some plants make seeds without flowers. Their seeds form in cones. **Cones** are the parts of some seed plants where reproduction occurs. Unlike flowers, cones do not develop into fruit. This pinecone has seeds in it that will grow into new pine trees.

Small Wonders

Big things can come in little packages! Did you know that even the tallest trees started out as small seeds?

Active Reading As you read these two pages, draw two lines under each main idea.

Plants that make seeds also make pollen. **Pollen** is a powder-like material involved in plant reproduction. **Pollination** happens when pollen is moved from the male plant part to the female plant part. The environment around a plant helps in pollination. Wind, water, and animals help move pollen from plant to plant. After a plant is pollinated, seeds form in the female parts of the flowers. The part of the flower that surrounds the seeds grows into a fruit. If a flower is not pollinated, it will not form seeds or grow fruit.

Insects and birds drink a sweet liquid called nectar from flowering plants. As they move from plant to plant, they carry pollen with them.

Many seeds have parts that float on the wind. Wind carries these lightweight dandelion seeds to new ground.

Seeds come in many shapes and sizes. When seeds are released from a plant, they are often carried to new areas. Water, wind, and animals carry seeds to new ground. When a seed lands in a good place, it grows into a new plant.

Do the Math!
Estimate an Answer

If 1 bee can pollinate 220 plants in 1 hour, estimate how many plants 9 bees can pollinate in the same amount of time.

one thoysind eight hyndrod

This fruit has seeds in it. If the bird eats the fruit, the seeds will pass through its body. The seeds may be left in a new place. This is one way seeds are spread.

More and More Spores

Plants with flowers make seeds. Plants with cones make seeds. Do all plants make seeds? Find out!

Active Reading As you read this page, draw a circle around a clue word that signals a comparison. Draw a box around a clue word that signals a contrast.

Some plants do not make flowers, cones, or seeds. Instead, they reproduce only with spores. Like seeds, **spores** are reproductive structures that can grow into new plants.

Ferns are one type of plant that reproduces using only spores. Ferns have leaves called *fronds*. Each frond has smaller leaves that branch off from the stem.

Spores form in small groups on the underside of the fern fronds. Each group contains hundreds of spores.

Moss is another type of plant that reproduces using only spores. Mosses are small, soft plants. Groups of moss often grow together in damp places without much light. Sometimes moss looks like a green blanket covering rocks and trees. This blanket is actually made up of many tiny moss plants.

Mosses make spores in little capsules at the end of stalks. The capsules keep the spores dry, while the moss remains damp. When the capsules dry out, they release the spores into the air. These tiny spores float away to make new plants where they land.

True or False

Read each statement. Circle *T* if the statement is true and *F* if it is false.

1. Spores are seeds. **T** F
2. Cones release spores. T **F**
3. Mosses make spores. **T** F
4. Ferns do not make flowers. T **F**
5. Mosses do not make seeds. **T** F

Sum It Up!

When you're done, use the answer key to check
and revise your work.

Write the vocabulary term that matches each photo and caption.

1
a sprout

This is what it's called when a
seed starts to grow.

2
cones

Some plants do not have flowers
to help them reproduce. Instead,
they have this plant part.

3
Drop seeds

This is what plants do to make
more plants.

4
pollen

This is what helps flowering
plants produce seeds.

Summarize

Fill in the missing words to tell about the life cycles of plants.

The different stages that a plant goes through in its life make up its

(5) _A seed_ . After a seed germinates, it becomes a

(6) _sprout_ . Insects are one way that (7) _helps seeds_

moves from a male plant part to a female plant part. In a flowering plant, the

(8) _____ contains the seeds that will grow into a new plant. Water,

wind, and (9) _____ carry seeds to new ground. Plants like mosses

make (10) _____ but do not make seeds when they reproduce.

Word Play

Name _____

1 Use the words in the box to complete the puzzle.

Across

3. The stages that a plant goes through in its life are called its ___life___.

5. The colorful part of a plant that helps it reproduce is called a _____.

7. When a seed ___grows___, it breaks open and a small plant grows out of it.

Down

1. _____ happens when pollen moves from the male part of a plant to a female part.

2. The powder-like material that helps plants reproduce is called _____.

4. Plants that make seeds but do not produce a fruit produce a _____.

6. When a seed plant _____, it makes seeds that will grow into new plants.

8. A _____ is the only structure that ferns use when they reproduce.

Across: 3. life cycle 5. flower 7. germinates
Down: 1. pollination 2. pollen 4. cone 6. reproduces 8. spore

~~life cycle*~~   ~~flower*~~   ~~reproduces*~~   ~~germinates*~~   pollination*   ~~pollen*~~
~~cone*~~   ~~spore*~~   *Key Lesson Vocabulary

Apply Concepts

2 Draw the life cycle of a peach tree. The first stage is already done.

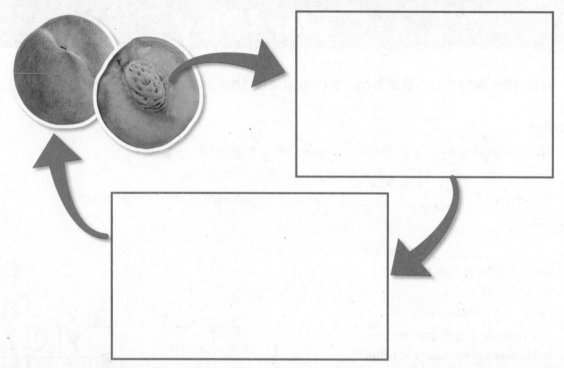

3 In each picture tell whether seeds or pollen are being moved.

_____ _____ _____

Take It Home!

Find out more about different types of seeds. Try planting three different types of seeds at home and observing the length of time they take to germinate. Also, pay attention to the amount of water and sunlight that the different seeds need.

What Are Some Animal Life Cycles?

Engage Your Brain!

Find the answer to the following question in this lesson and record it here.

Why does this young koala look similar to its mother?

_____

_____

_____

Active Reading

Lesson Vocabulary

List the terms. As you learn about each one, make notes in the Interactive Glossary.

_____ _____

_____ _____

Sequence

Many ideas in this lesson are connected by a sequence, or order, that describes the steps in a process. Active readers stay focused on sequence when they mark the transition from one step in a process to another.

Life Cycles

Robins hatch from eggs. Dogs give birth to live puppies. What do dogs and robins have in common?

Active Reading As you read these two pages, circle words that show differences between animal life cycles.

Most animals have male and female parents. But not all animals *reproduce*, or have young, in the same way. Birds and some fish, reptiles, and amphibians lay eggs. Other animals, such as mammals, give birth to live young. These early stages are part of each animal's life cycle.

Newborn lynx
A mother lynx gives birth to live cubs. There can be one to four cubs in a litter.

Ostrich egg
The ostrich is the largest bird. It's not surprising that ostriches lay very large eggs.

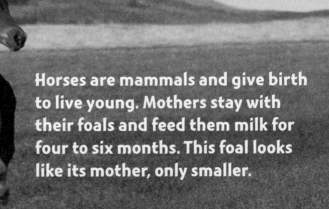

Horses are mammals and give birth to live young. Mothers stay with their foals and feed them milk for four to six months. This foal looks like its mother, only smaller.

Lynx cub

A young lynx grows up in the protection of its mother. A young lynx looks much like its parents, only smaller.

Adult lynx

A young lynx grows into an adult and finds a mate. The two adult lynxes reproduce.

Newborn lynx

The cycle begins again with a new litter of lynx cubs.

Ostrich chick

An ostrich chick depends on its mother to bring it food.

Adult ostrich

All grown up, an adult female can find a mate and reproduce.

What's Next?

Draw the next stage in the ostrich life cycle.

Frog Life Cycle

A frog is sitting beside a pond, croaking loudly. How did it get there? How has it changed?

Active Reading As you read these two pages, circle words that name stages in the frog's life cycle.

Early in the spring, many frogs wake from hibernation and begin to croak. They are looking for mates. Before long, the pond's water is filled with eggs. Look closely at the photo of a clump of frog eggs. You will see tiny black specks. One day, each speck will grow into a frog as big and green as the one on this page. As a frog develops, its entire appearance changes. **Metamorphosis** [met•uh•MAWR•fuh•sis] is a major change in the body form of an animal during its life cycle.

Egg mass

Frog eggs are found all stuck together. They look like a cloud of eggs. They are usually in the water of a pond or marsh.

(**Leopard frog**)

The leopard frog goes through a series of changes after it hatches as a tadpole.

Tadpole

A tadpole is an immature frog that must live in the water. It hatches from an egg. It has gills and a long tail. It breathes and swims like a fish. It looks very different from its parents.

Life Cycles

How is the life cycle of a frog different from the life cycle of an ostrich?

_____

_____

_____

_____

_____

After about five weeks, the tadpole starts to change. Tiny buds beside the tadpole's tail grow into little hind legs.

Still a tadpole, this young frog has four legs. Its tail will soon disappear. Its lungs are almost completely developed.

Adult frog

This frog has fully developed legs and lungs. There are no gills and no tail. It's an adult!

Insect Life Cycles

Ladybugs crawl up a brick wall. Grasshoppers hop along the ground. What changes did these insects go through after they hatched from eggs?

Active Reading As you read this page, circle a signal word that tells when something happens.

Most insects undergo metamorphosis as they develop into adults. Ladybugs, like butterflies, go through complete metamorphosis. This means that they go through two stages of development between the egg and the adult. In both of these stages, the insect looks very different from the adult.

Some insects, such as grasshoppers and dragonflies, go through incomplete metamorphosis. After hatching, these insects look very much like adult insects. They also go through changes as they grow, but the way they look does not change much.

Complete Metamorphosis

Ladybug eggs

An adult ladybug lays her eggs on a leaf. The egg is the first stage in complete metamorphosis.

Incomplete Metamorphosis

Grasshopper eggs

A grasshopper lays her eggs in the soil. The egg is the first stage of incomplete metamorphosis.

As part of its life cycle, the adult grasshopper grows bigger and gains wings.

Ladybug larva

In the second stage, a ladybug larva hatches from each egg. The larva looks different from the adult.

Ladybug pupa

The larva becomes a pupa. During this third stage, the insect does not move as it slowly changes into an adult.

Adult ladybug

An adult ladybug emerges. The adult stage is the last of the four stages of complete metamorphosis.

Grasshopper nymph

Young grasshoppers, called *nymphs* [NIMFS], hatch from the eggs. A nymph looks like an adult grasshopper, but it doesn't have wings.

Grasshopper nymph

As a nymph grows, it sheds its outer body covering several times. Each time, its wings become larger and more fully formed.

Adult grasshopper

The last shedding produces an adult grasshopper. This is the third and last stage of incomplete metamorphosis.

Do the Math!
Measure in Millimeters

A young grasshopper nymph can be 20 millimeters long. Draw a nymph that is 20 millimeters long.

An adult grasshopper can be 45 millimeters long. Draw a grasshopper that is 45 millimeters long.

Diversity

Every living thing is different. Even young who have the same parents are not the same.

Imagine a family of dogs. The mother has brown fur. The father has black fur. What color fur will the puppies have? The answer may be different for every single puppy. Even though they have the same parents, they will get different features from each parent.

All living things share traits, or similar characteristics, with their parents. Hair and eye color are passed on from parents. Even talents and abilities may be passed on from parents to their children.

A family of dogs

These puppies have the same parents, but they all look different. That's because they have received different features from their parents.

Members of the same family often share the same features. Think about families you know. Which features do they share? Which features are different?

Look at the family in the photo on these pages. Do the members of the family look alike? People with the same parents often look alike. But they don't look exactly alike. *Diversity*—different characteristics— is what makes everyone different from one another.

Comparing Puppies

Circle two puppies. Compare their similarities and differences.

_____

_____

_____

_____

_____

_____

109

Sum It Up!

When you're done, use the answer key to check
and revise your work.

**The blue part of each statement is incorrect. Write words to replace
the blue parts.**

1 Most reptiles have live births.

_____

2 Ostriches and other birds lay puppies.

_____

3 Tadpoles look exactly like adult frogs.

_____

4 Nymphs hatch from frog eggs.

_____

5 Ladybugs go through incomplete metamorphosis.

_____

6 The stages of the ladybug life cycle are egg, larva, tadpole, adult.

_____

7 A young grasshopper is called a larva.

_____

8 One way a nymph is different from an adult grasshopper is that it has no legs.

_____

Answer Key: 1. mammals 2. eggs 3. very little 4. Tadpoles 5. complete 6. pupa 7. nymph 8. wings

Name _____

Word Play

1 Use the words in the box to complete the puzzle.

Across

4. A ladybug egg hatches and a _____ comes out.

6. Through _____, a tadpole becomes an adult frog.

8. During complete metamorphosis, a larva becomes a _____.

9. A _____ cycle includes many stages in an organism's life.

Down

1. After the pupa stage, a ladybug is an _____.

2. A _____ is an immature form of a frog.

3. Most birds and reptiles _____ by laying eggs.

5. _____ allow a tadpole to breathe under water.

7. Birds lay an _____ as part of their life cycle.

metamorphosis*	larva*	tadpole*	pupa*	gills	life
egg		reproduce	adult		

*Key Lesson Vocabulary

Apply Concepts

2 Show the life cycle for each animal below. You may draw or write your answer in the boxes provided.

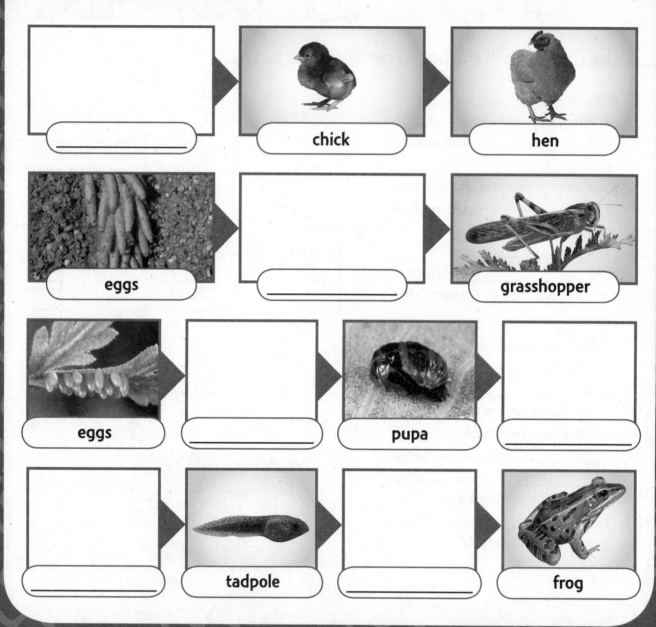

_____

chick

hen

eggs

_____

grasshopper

eggs

_____

pupa

_____

_____

tadpole

_____

frog

Take It Home! With your family, talk about animal life cycles. Walk in your neighborhood. For one animal you see, tell the stages of its life cycle. If you do not know, research it.

Name _____

Essential Question

How Do Living Things Change?

Set a Purpose

In this activity, you will observe plant seeds several times. Why do you think scientists make many observations?

_____

_____

_____

_____

Think About the Procedure

Why do you think that placing the seeds on a sunny windowsill and watering them is part of the procedure?

_____

_____

_____

_____

How can you make sure you are measuring the growth of the plant accurately?

_____

_____

_____

_____

Record Your Data

Use your data table to draw a line graph below that shows how your plant grew over time.

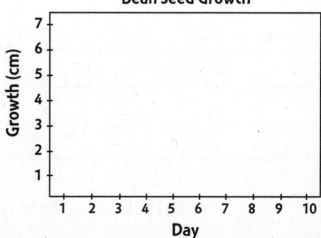

Bean Seed Growth

Draw Conclusions

What did you observe? Infer why the
seeds responded this way.

_____

_____

_____

_____

_____

_____

Analyze and Extend

1. Compare your observations with
   those of classmates. Did everyone
   have the same results? Why or
   why not?

_____

_____

_____

_____

_____

_____

_____

2. What do you think will happen to
   the plants if you do not water
   them for the next 10 days? What if
   you move the plants off the
   sunny windowsill?

_____

_____

_____

_____

_____

_____

_____

3. Think of other questions you
   would like to ask about the way
   seeds grow.

_____

_____

_____

_____

_____

_____

Essential Question

What Are Structural Adaptations?

Engage Your Brain!

Find the answer to the following question in this lesson and record it here.

Why is the pelican's beak so large?

_____

_____

_____

_____

Active Reading

Lesson Vocabulary

List the terms. As you learn about each one, make notes in the Interactive Glossary.

_____

_____

_____

Visual Aids

Pictures and their captions add information to the text on a page. Active readers pause their reading to review pictures and captions, then decide how the information in the pictures and captions adds to what is provided in the text.

Staying Alive

Life in the wild isn't easy. Animals must survive in the environment where they live. Their adaptations help them stay alive.

Active Reading As you read these two pages, draw a line from the adaptation shown in each picture to the words that describe it.

An **adaptation** is any trait that helps a living thing survive. Animals that are hunted for food are called *prey*. Animals that hunt prey are called *predators.* Predators and prey have adaptations that help them catch food or avoid being eaten. Animals have other kinds of adaptations, too.

What animal is this? It has flat teeth. The flat teeth allow it to grind grass.

The tiger eats animals such as wild boar and deer. The tiger's sharp teeth help it tear meat.

The arctic hare lives in snow and ice. Less heat escapes from its small ears than from the larger ears of other hares. Its small ears help it stay warm in the cold.

The jackrabbit lives in the desert. Its long ears contain many tiny blood vessels that help remove heat from its body. This helps the jackrabbit keep cool in the heat.

Guess Who?

A finch has a beak that it uses to crack seeds and nuts. An eagle uses its beak to tear meat for food. Which bird's beak is shown in photo 1? In photo 2?

1. _____

2. _____

Staying Safe

Look out! It's a predator! Some adaptations help animals defend themselves without fighting.

Active Reading As you read these two pages, find and underline examples of defense adaptations.

Defense adaptations may attack a predator's sense of sight, smell, taste, touch, or hearing. A bad taste, loud noise, or nasty odor is often enough to make the predator go away.

A porcupine raises its quills. It swings its tail. One good strike pokes the quills into the attacker's skin. Ouch!

A skunk's spray has a bad odor. Even skunks dislike the smell! The spray also burns the eyes. It's a powerful defense against predators.

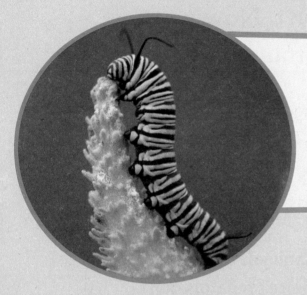

This caterpillar eats milkweed. The milkweed makes the caterpillar taste bad to birds. The pattern of stripes on the caterpillar is a warning to birds. It tells the birds that they don't want to eat it.

The frilled lizard hisses with open jaws. Its frill opens wide. It's a scary sight that frightens some predators away.

Sound the Alarm!

Like pet dogs, prairie dogs bark when they sense danger. How does this adaptation help them survive?

_____

_____

Creature Costumes

Now you see it. Now you don't. Now you see it—but it looks like something else!

Active Reading As you read these two pages, find and underline the names of two adaptations that involve an animal's appearance.

Some animals can hide without trying. These animals are hidden by their shapes, colors, or patterns. Such disguises are called **camouflage** [KAM•uh•flazh].

Some harmless animals look a lot like animals that are harmful to predators or that taste bad. Since predators don't know which animal is harmful, neither animal gets eaten. Imitating the look of another animal is called **mimicry**.

Look at the color of this snow leopard's fur. Look at its spots. Its camouflage helps it blend into the background of snow and rock. This helps it sneak up on prey.

This orchid mantis is the same color as the flower it's sitting on. The insect is perfectly camouflaged!

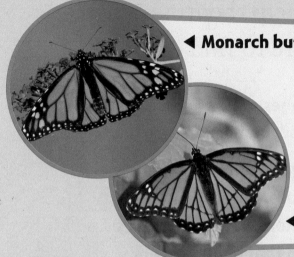

◄ **Monarch butterfly**

Eating monarch butterflies makes birds sick. Birds avoid eating them. The viceroy looks like the monarch, so birds leave them alone, too.

◄ **Viceroy butterfly**

The frogfish can look like a rock or a sponge. It can look like algae. Animals try to rest on the "rock." Others try to eat the "algae." The frogfish traps and eats them!

Make It Blend!

Color the lizard so that it is hidden on the leaf. On the line below, identify whether this is camouflage or mimicry.

_____

Plant Facts

Plants have adaptations that help them survive, too. How? Read more to find out!

Active Reading As you read these two pages, draw a line from the pictures to the words that tell how an adaptation helps a plant.

Plants need water. There isn't much water in a desert, so desert plants are adapted to hold moisture. Desert plants such as cactuses have thick stems that store water. The leaves of desert plants also have a waxy coating that helps prevent water loss. Most desert plants have spines, not leaves. Narrow spines help prevent water vapor from escaping from the plant. The spines also keep animals from eating the plants. Other plants have different adaptations that help them survive.

Pitcher plants can't get the nutrients they need from soil. The plants' pitchers hold water and trap insects for food. The sides are slippery, so when insects fall into the pitchers, they can't get out! The insects are digested, providing nutrients to the plant.

Blackberries taste bitter until they are ripe. Their bitter taste is an adaptation. It stops animals from eating the berries before the seeds are old enough to produce new plants.

The stone plant blends into the background of rocks and stones. Grazing animals don't see it. Camouflage keeps it from being eaten.

Do the Math!
Solve a Word Problem

A red pitcher plant catches 3 insects each week. A green pitcher plant catches 2 insects each week. How many more insects does the red plant catch in four weeks than the green plant? Show your work.

_____

_____

_____

_____

Sum It Up!

When you're done, use the answer key to
check and revise your work.

Complete the summary. Use it to complete the graphic organizer.

Summarize

(1) _____
are characteristics that help living
things survive.

(2) _____
is a kind of adaptation. It helps the
frogfish blend into algae and catch
prey. An adaptation called

(3) _____ makes
the harmless viceroy butterfly look
like the harmful monarch butterfly.

**Main Idea: Living things have adaptations that help them survive
in their environments.**

(4) Detail:	(5) Detail:	Detail: A horse has flat teeth to help it grind grass.

protects the viceroy butterfly from predators.
Camouflage helps the frogfish stay hidden from prey. 5. Sample answer: Mimicry
Answer Key: 1. Adaptations 2. Camouflage 3. mimicry 4. Sample answer:

Word Play

1

Unscramble the letters to complete each clue.	
1. _____ help living things survive in their environments.	p i d t a t a n a o s
2. Some plants have adaptations that help _____ them against animals that eat them.	f e d d e n
3. _____ helps an animal blend into its surroundings.	f a m a l o g c u e
4. An adaptation that makes one organism look like another is called _____.	y i m r m c i
5. A porcupine's _____ protect it from other animals.	s i l u q l
6. Animals do not eat the _____ butterfly because it looks like the monarch butterfly.	c o i r e y v

Apply Concepts

2 Look at each picture. Write the kind of adaptation that it shows.

_____

_____

3 Draw two pictures. Show an adaptation of a plant. Show an adaptation of an animal. Write captions to describe your pictures.

Plant Adaptation

Animal Adaptation

_____

_____

_____

_____

_____

_____

Take It Home!

Observe a plant or animal in its natural habitat. What is one of its adaptations? How does the adaptation help it survive?

Meet the Insect Scientists

Miriam Rothschild 1908–2005

As a child, Miriam Rothschild collected beetles and caterpillars. Later, she studied fleas and other parasites. Parasites are living things that live on or in other living things. Rothschild studied fleas on rabbits' fur. She discovered how fleas jump. In 1952, she wrote her first book. It was called *Fleas, Flukes and Cuckoos*. In 1973, she finished a book about 30,000 different fleas.

Rothschild studied the life cycle of the flea and how it reproduces.

Charles Henry Turner 1867–1923

Charles Turner was an entomologist, a scientist who studies insects. He studied many kinds of insects, including ants and honeybees. In 1910, he proved that honeybees can see color. The next year he proved they could also see patterns. Turner found that some ants move in circles toward their home. To honor his work with ants, scientists call this behavior "Turner's circling."

Turner showed that honeybees can see a flower's color.

The Insect Scientists

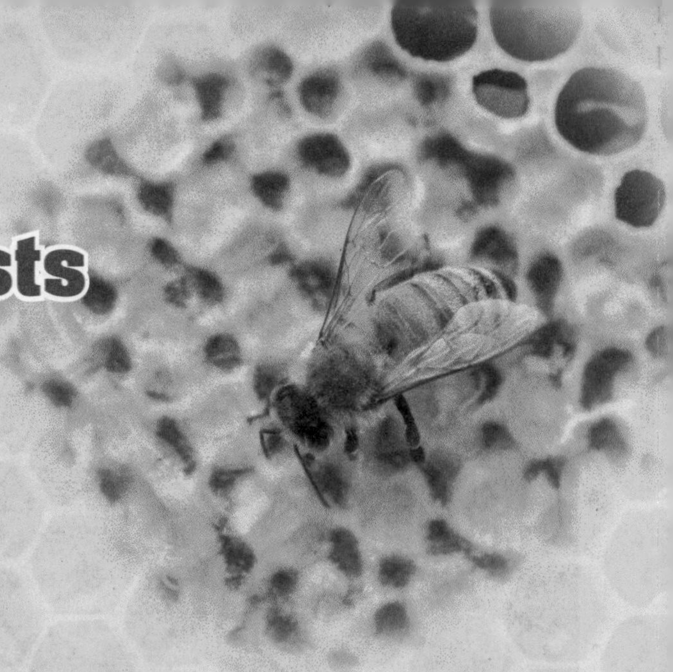

Read the timeline below. Use what you read about Rothschild and Turner to fill in each blank box.

_____

_____

_____

1952 Rothschild writes her first book.

1910 Turner proves that honeybees can see color.

1908 Miriam Rothschild is born.

_____

_____

_____

1907 Charles Turner writes about his study of ants.

Think About It!

After what year on the timeline should you add the following?

A scientist names the circles that ants make when returning home "Turner's circling."

_____

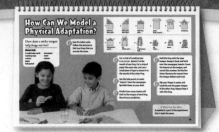

Name _____

Essential Question

How Can We Model a Physical Adaptation?

Set a Purpose
What will you learn from this experiment?

_____

_____

_____

Think About the Procedure
How do you think the stickiness of the tongue will affect the number of insects the frog catches? State your prediction.

_____

_____

_____

Why do you think the pieces of paper are all the same size?

_____

_____

_____

_____

Record Your Data

Record the number of insects caught with a sticky tongue and with a wet tongue for each of your five trials.

Trial	1	2	3	4	5
Sticky tongue					
Wet tongue					

Draw Conclusions

Which is better at catching insects: a sticky tongue or a wet tongue? Why?

_____

_____

_____

_____

Analyze and Extend

1. How is a sticky tongue an example of an adaptation?

_____

_____

_____

_____

_____

2. How would this experiment change if the insects were inside a test tube instead of on the flat desktop?

_____

_____

_____

3. Suppose you were an insect that lived in an area with many sticky-tongued frogs. What adaptation might help you survive?

_____

_____

_____

_____

_____

4. What kind of tongue is better for catching insects? What other animals do you think might have this kind of tongue?

_____

_____

_____

_____

5. What other questions do you have about adaptations for eating?

_____

_____

_____

_____

Essential Question

What Are Behavioral Adaptations?

Engage Your Brain!

Find the answer to the following question in this lesson and record it here.

Migrating geese often fly in a V formation. How do they know when it is time to migrate?

_____

_____

_____

Active Reading

Lesson Vocabulary

List the terms. As you learn about each one, make notes in the Interactive Glossary.

_____ _____

_____ _____

_____

Compare and Contrast

Many ideas in this lesson are connected because they show comparisons and contrasts—how things are alike and how things are different. Active readers stay focused on comparisons and contrasts by asking themselves, How are these things alike? How are these things different?

Know It or Learn It?

Eating, sleeping, finding shelter, and moving from place to place. How do animals know what to do?

Active Reading As you read these two pages, circle words that tell how instinct and learned behaviors are different. Underline examples of each.

A **behavior** is anything an organism does. **Learned behaviors** are behaviors that come from watching other animals or through experience. Young animals learn how to behave by watching and copying adults.

There are other behaviors. An **instinct** is a behavior that an animal knows without learning it. Animals are born with instincts. Behaviors are adaptations that may help an animal survive in its environment.

A mother lion teaches her cubs to hunt. Searching for food is an instinct. Knowing how to find and catch food is something cubs learn by copying their parents.

A mother sea turtle buries her eggs in the sand. Most young sea turtles hatch at night. Their instinct is to go toward the brightest area. This instinct helps the hatchlings find the ocean.

A chimpanzee isn't born knowing how to use a tool. It learns this behavior by watching others. Sometimes, a chimp may figure it out on its own.

It is an instinct for some birds to sing, but sometimes the songs they sing are learned from other birds.

A spider's web helps it survive. The web is sticky, so it traps insects. But how does a spider know how to spin a web? This is an instinctive behavior.

A moth's instinct is to use moonlight to find its way. That is why moths are attracted to porch lights.

► How are instincts and learned behaviors alike?

_____

_____

_____

_____

Finding Food

Hungry. Cold. Wet. That's what animals would be without the instinct to find food and shelter.

Active Reading As you read these two pages, underline details that tell ways animals find food. Circle ways animals find shelter.

Every animal looks for food when it's hungry. It's an instinctual behavior. But actually finding food can be a learned behavior. Some animals learn from watching their parents or other adults. But some animals can learn by themselves, too.

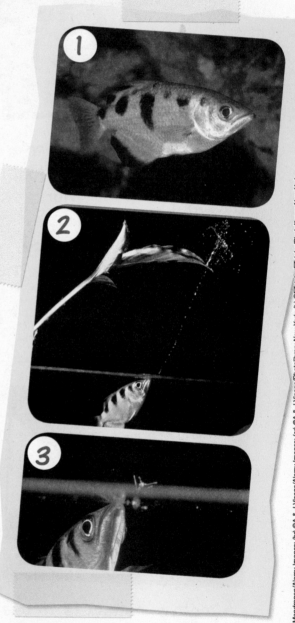

Bears come to this stream to catch salmon. The bears wait for the fish to swim upstream. This is a learned behavior.

How did this archerfish know how to get food from above the water? The fish instinctively shoots water at insects in the air to catch them.

Finding Shelter

These birds learned to build nests on buildings when trees were cut down.

A gopher uses what it has—soil and claws—to make a shelter in the ground.

How Animals Survive

How does building an anthill help the group of ants?

_____

_____

_____

_____

_____

_____

Ants work together to make an anthill. They use the soil around them. The hill hides a tunnel system that provides shelter and storage space for food.

Hibernation

When the weather turns cold, it is time for many animals to slow down.

As you read these two pages, draw a line under the words that describe what is happening to the animals in the photos.

Animals respond to cold winter weather in different ways. Some animals stay active during winter. They find food or eat food they have hidden. Other animals **hibernate**, or go into a deep, sleeplike state that helps them survive the cold winter conditions. Normal body activities slow down. The heart beats slowly, and breathing almost stops. Hibernating is an instinctive behavior.

A hibernating animal doesn't use much energy, because its body is barely working. There is enough fat stored in the animal's body to keep it alive through the winter.

This ground squirrel spent the fall eating and gaining weight. It stored up enough energy to survive winter hibernation. The squirrel's heart rate and breathing have become slower.

Many bats like this one hibernate in the winter. In the spring when the weather warms up, there is more food for the bat. It will come out of hibernation.

Which animals hibernate? Many animals that eat insects hibernate. These animals include bats, hedgehogs, and hamsters. Insects such as ladybugs and bees also hibernate. So do lizards, snakes, turtles, skunks, badgers, and many more animals.

These snakes are all hibernating together. When spring arrives, they will leave this den.

Look at the Data

How does each animal's heart rate change during hibernation?

Animal's Heart Rate	Bat	Woodchuck
Non-hibernation	450 beats per minute	160 beats per minute
Hibernation	40 beats per minute	4 beats per minute

_____

_____

Migration

Some animals are travelers. Some whales make a yearly trip from someplace cold to someplace warm and back.

Active Reading As you read, compare the different reasons animals migrate. Circle each reason an animal might migrate.

Animals **migrate** when they move a long distance as a group from one region to another and back. Whales swim to a warm place to mate. They swim to a different spot to give birth. Then they swim back to where they were to find food.

Many animals, including birds and fish, migrate. Whales and some other animals teach their young the way to go. The path the animals take is learned, but knowing when to migrate is an instinct.

Gray whales have one of the longest migration routes of any mammal. They travel up to 21,000 kilometers each year. Gray whales swim from the cold Arctic to warm Mexico to have their young.

In the winter, when the land freezes over in the Arctic, tundra swans fly to the warmer south. When the weather warms up, the swans return to the Arctic. There, they mate and wait for their eggs to hatch.

© Houghton Mifflin Harcourt Publishing Company   (t) ©Francois Gohier/Adea London Limited; (b) ©Chris Gomersall/Alamy Images

Migration Routes of Gray Whales and Tundra Swans

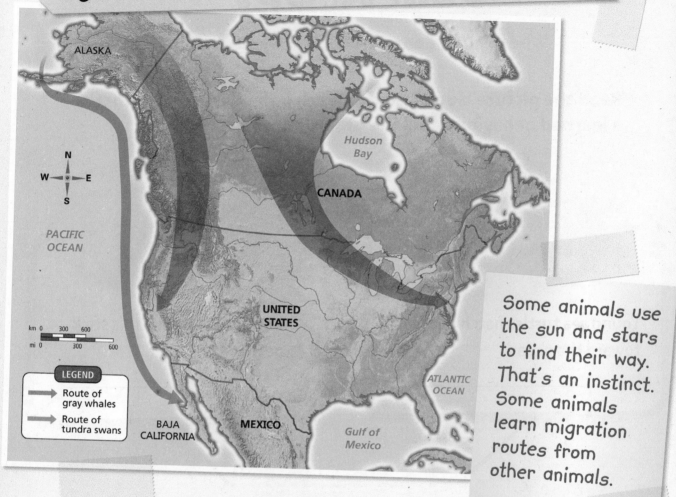

Some animals use the sun and stars to find their way. That's an instinct. Some animals learn migration routes from other animals.

Do the Math!
Make a Graph

Many animals migrate. The gray whale may travel over 10,000 kilometers each way as it migrates. The tundra swan may travel over 3,000 kilometers each way as it migrates. Draw a bar graph to compare the distances.

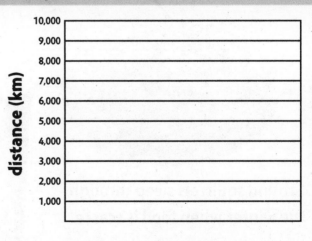

Sum It Up!

Read the picture clues. Decide if each behavior is an instinct or a learned behavior. Label the graphic organizer.

1

Young sea turtles hatch and walk toward the ocean.

_____

2

Chimps use tools like this stick to get food.

_____

Behavioral Adaptations

3

Ground squirrels sleep through the winter when food is scarce.

_____

4

Grizzly bears wait in the water to catch fish.

_____

Answer Key: 1. instinct 2. learned behavior 3. instinct 4. learned behavior

Name _____

Word Play

1 Use the words in the box to complete the puzzle.

adaptations	behavior*	instinct*	learn
migrate*	parent	shelter	hibernate*

* Key Lesson Vocabulary

Across

4. Behaviors are _____ that help organisms survive.

7. Animals that _____ enjoy a long winter's rest.

8. Animals _____ to hunt by watching other animals.

Down

1. A young animal learns behaviors by watching its _____.

2. Animals that need a warm place out of the rain seek _____.

3. Looking for food and shelter is an _____.

5. Each year, gray whales _____ thousands of miles.

6. Migration and hibernation are two examples of animal _____.

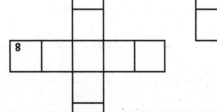

141

Apply Concepts

2 How are instincts and learned behaviors the same? What is the difference between them?

_____

_____

_____

_____

3 Look at the photos. Write how the behavior helps the animal survive.

_____ _____ _____ _____

_____ _____ _____ _____

_____ _____ _____ _____

_____ _____ _____ _____

Talk to your family about the things you do every day. Which things have you learned? Which are instincts?

Save It for Later:
Food Preservation

Long ago, people learned to save, or preserve, food. First, people used nature to help them preserve food. Then, people made tools and processes to help. Follow the timeline to see how food preservation has changed over time.

5,000 Years Ago

Salt preserved meat. Ice kept food from spoiling. People dried meat and fruit.

1795

Heating foods in glass jars kept them fresh. Preserving foods in glass jars and metal cans became common.

1855

In an icebox, air flowed around a block of ice like this one. The cool air kept food fresh.

What types of food preservation are still used today? Why are older ways still used even though we have newer tools?

_____

_____

_____

Analyze a Product

Grocery stores are filled with products that are preserved for freshness. Think about a favorite product you buy in the grocery store.

Frozen dinners last about six months.

1900s

Refrigerators became common in the 1940s. Before the 1990s, most refrigerators used gases that harmed the atmosphere.

How is your favorite product preserved? How does the package help it stay fresh? How long does it last after you open it?

_____

_____

_____

Build On It!

Rise to the engineering design challenge—complete **Solve It: Helping Animals Migrate** on the Inquiry Flipchart.

Unit 3 Review

Name _____

Vocabulary Review

Use the terms in the box to complete the sentences.

adaptation
behavior
germinate
life cycle
metamorphosis

1. A frog develops front and back legs during
   _____.

2. A bird building a nest is an example of a(n)
   _____.

3. Before a new plant can grow, the seed must
   _____.

4. Snakes lay eggs as part of their _____.

5. The quill of a porcupine is a structural _____.

Science Concepts

Fill in the letter of the choice that best answers the question.

6. What happens when a plant is pollinated?

   Ⓐ Pollen is brought from the male part of the plant to the female part.

   Ⓑ New roots start to grow and begin absorbing water.

   Ⓒ A seed germinates and begins to sprout.

   Ⓓ A spore forms from a seed.

7. Look at the butterfly life cycle.

   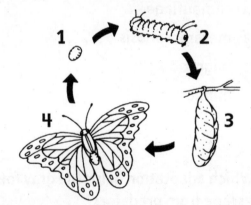

   What stage is being shown at step 3 in the diagram?

   Ⓐ adult   Ⓒ larva

   Ⓑ egg   Ⓓ pupa

Science Concepts

Fill in the letter of the choice that best answers the question.

8. Animals have many behaviors. Some are learned and some come from instinct. Which of the following behaviors is based on instinct?

   Ⓐ a chimpanzee using a tool to dig up insects

   Ⓑ bats hibernating in the winter months

   Ⓒ lion cubs imitating hunting behaviors of their mother

   Ⓓ a dog responding to its owner's commands

9. Oscar enjoys bird watching. His favorite bird is a warbler, but he can see them only during the month of September. After that, the warblers head south in search of food. What is the warbler's behavior an example of?

   Ⓐ camouflage

   Ⓑ metamorphosis

   Ⓒ migration

   Ⓓ mimicry

10. Which adaptation helps the gray fox to escape from predators?

   Ⓐ It has thick fur.

   Ⓑ It reproduces in the spring.

   Ⓒ It goes through hibernation.

   Ⓓ It has the ability to climb trees.

11. Animals have body structures that help them to find food and shelter or defend themselves from predators. Look at the picture below.

   What adaptation helps the cheetah compete with other animals for food?

   Ⓐ climbing ability

   Ⓑ a long life cycle

   Ⓒ fur to maintain body heat

   Ⓓ strong legs for high-speed hunting

12. Flowers come in many shapes, sizes, and colors. How is this a plant adaptation?

   Ⓐ The different flowers help make a garden look attractive.

   Ⓑ The different flowers help the plant get the most sunlight.

   Ⓒ The different flower types help the plant survive in different climates.

   Ⓓ The different flower types attract different kinds of insects to pollinate them.

13. Tanisha is making a chart about the life cycle of a pine tree. Place the stages of the tree's life cycle below in the correct sequence.

> 1. A seed forms inside a cone.
>
> 2. A plant grows into an adult pine tree.
>
> 3. Pollen goes from a male cone to a female cone.
>
> 4. A seed germinates and a new plant sprouts.

(A) 1, 2, 3, 4

(B) 3, 1, 4, 2

(C) 2, 1, 4, 3

(D) 4, 3, 2, 1

14. Austin has a female yellow and white cat that just had kittens. The father of the kittens is a black cat. The litter of kittens contains three black kittens, two yellow kittens, and one kitten that is black, yellow, and white. How can you explain these results?

(A) There is no way of telling what the offspring of an animal will look like.

(B) The male kittens are probably all black and the other cats are females.

(C) Each kitten got a different mix of features from the mother and father cats.

(D) The kittens' fur will get darker and they soon will all have black fur.

15. A scientist is studying the behavior of chipmunks. She records the information below.

Month	Average Body Temperature (°F)
January	55
April	90
June	99
October	95

Which adaptation is shown in the graph above?

(A) camouflage

(C) migration

(B) hibernation

(D) mimicry

16. Which part of a cactus allows it to survive long periods of dry weather?

(A) It has very shallow roots.

(B) It has large, colorful flowers.

(C) It has thick stems to hold extra water.

(D) It has thin, sharp needles.

17. The male snowy owl is almost completely white. It lives near the Arctic Circle, where this adaptation helps it stay hidden while hunting. What type of adaptation is this?

(A) camouflage

(C) instinct

(B) hibernation

(D) mimicry

Apply Inquiry and Review the Big Idea

Write the answers to these questions.

18. Matt is investigating the life cycle of plants. He wants to see if squash seeds germinate and grow faster than bean seeds. Design an experiment he can do to find out. Identify the controls, the variable, and the hypothesis. Then describe how you would display the results.

_____

_____

_____

_____

_____

_____

_____

19. Katerina is doing a project on adaptations in birds for the science fair. Explain how she could use the materials shown here as models to show how different birds are adapted to eating different foods.

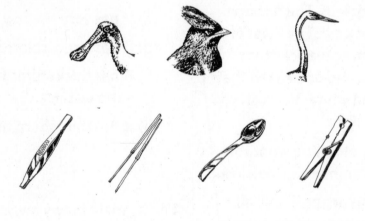

_____

_____

_____

Ecosystems and Interactions

Acacia ants live in bull-horn acacia trees.

Big Idea

All the living, once-living, and nonliving things interact in an ecosystem. All living things need energy to survive and grow.

I Wonder Why

Why does this acacia ant live in a bull-horn acacia tree? *Turn the page to find out.*

Here's why Acacia ants get food from the tree. In return, the ants protect the tree against animals and plants that are harmful to the tree.

In this unit, you will explore the Big Idea, the Essential Questions, and the Investigations on the Inquiry Flipchart.

Science Notebook

Before you begin each lesson, be sure to write your thoughts about the Essential Question.

Essential Question

What Are Ecosystems?

Engage Your Brain!

Find the answer to the following question in this lesson and record it here.

This woodpecker stores acorns in this tree. Why is the tree part of the woodpecker's habitat?

_____

_____

_____

Active Reading

Lesson Vocabulary

List the terms. As you learn about each one, make notes in the Interactive Glossary.

_____ _____

_____ _____

_____

Main Idea and Details

Detail sentences give information about a topic. The information may be examples, features, characteristics, or facts. Active readers stay focused on the topic when they ask, What fact or information does this sentence add to the topic?

Animals and Plants at Home

What do sand, salt water, crabs, and seaweed all have in common? You can find them at the beach, of course!

Active Reading As you read these two pages, draw two lines under each main idea.

When you go to the beach, you find lots of living things. Nonliving things, like sand and salt water, are also part of the beach. Everything that surrounds a living thing is its **environment**. This includes living and nonliving things. Your desk, teacher, books, and air are all part of your classroom environment.

An **ecosystem** is all of the living and nonliving things in a place. In an ecosystem, living things interact with each other and with the nonliving parts of their environment. Think of bees that use an old log to build their hive. They gather nectar from flowers to make honey. A bear eats the honey. These interactions make up a part of an ecosystem.

Living things in the same ecosystem share resources. Many of them also share a habitat. A **habitat** is the space where a plant or animal lives. A frog's habitat is a pond. A frog's environment is everything around the frog.

This crab's habitat is on the sand. The crab and sand are both part of an ecosystem.

© Houghton Mifflin Harcourt Publishing Company   (inset) ©Serge Vero/Alamy   (bg) ©Pere Sanz/Alamy Images

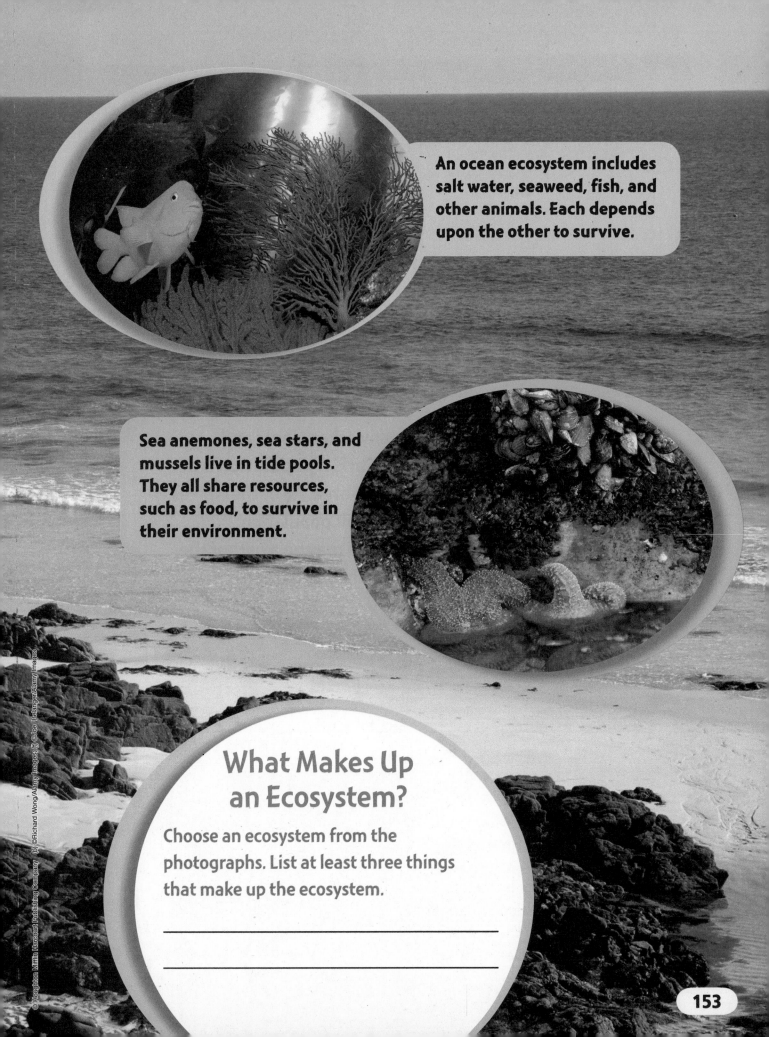

An ocean ecosystem includes salt water, seaweed, fish, and other animals. Each depends upon the other to survive.

Sea anemones, sea stars, and mussels live in tide pools. They all share resources, such as food, to survive in their environment.

What Makes Up an Ecosystem?

Choose an ecosystem from the photographs. List at least three things that make up the ecosystem.

_____

_____

Communities of Populations

You live in a community. You are also part of a population. Animals and plants are part of populations in communities, too.

Active Reading As you read these two pages, find and underline an example of a population.

Wolves, bears, snakes, birds, and many other plants and animals all live in Yellowstone National Park. A **population** is all of one kind of organism living in the same area. All of the wolves in Yellowstone National Park make up a wolf population.

Animal and plant populations in an area may be a part of the same community. A **community** is all of the populations that live and interact in an area. An ecosystem can have many different communities.

Grassland Ecosystem

Yellowstone National Park has a large population of bison. The bison are part of a community that includes the grasses that bison eat and this population of antelope.

© Houghton Mifflin Harcourt Publishing Company (bg) ©Joe Austin Photography/Alamy Images; (inset) ©Jana Thompson/Alamy Images

This bull snake is also part of the Yellowstone National Park community along with the wolves and bison.

This wolf is a part of the wolf population that lives in the same area. To survive, wolves eat other animals in their community.

Do the Math!
Make a Bar Graph

Use the data in the table to create a bar graph to compare populations of animals in a community within Yellowstone National Park.

Animal	Population
Bald Eagle	5
Gray Wolf	35
Elk	70
Bull Snake	15

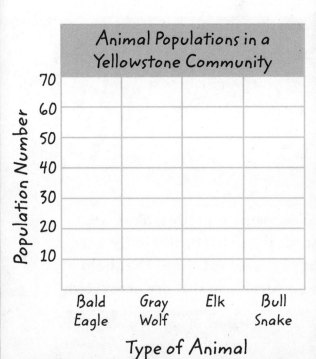

Animal Populations in a Yellowstone Community

Population Number

70
60
50
40
30
20
10

Bald Eagle   Gray Wolf   Elk   Bull Snake

Type of Animal

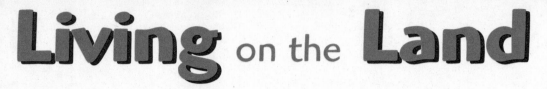
Living on the Land

You've seen that bison live in grassland ecosystems. What other types of land ecosystems are there?

Active Reading As you read these two pages, draw circles around the names of ecosystems that are described.

Forest ecosystems have a lot of trees. Tropical rain forests have many different kinds of trees. These forests are warm and wet all year long. Animals like jaguars, toucans, and monkeys live in tropical forests.

Some forests have warm summers and cold winters. Woodpeckers, squirrels, deer, and bears are common. The trees, such as oaks and maples, lose their leaves in the fall.

Other land ecosystems are shown on these two pages.

Desert Ecosystem
Kangaroo rats, rattlesnakes, and cactus populations live in deserts. They have adaptations that help them survive in this dry ecosystem.

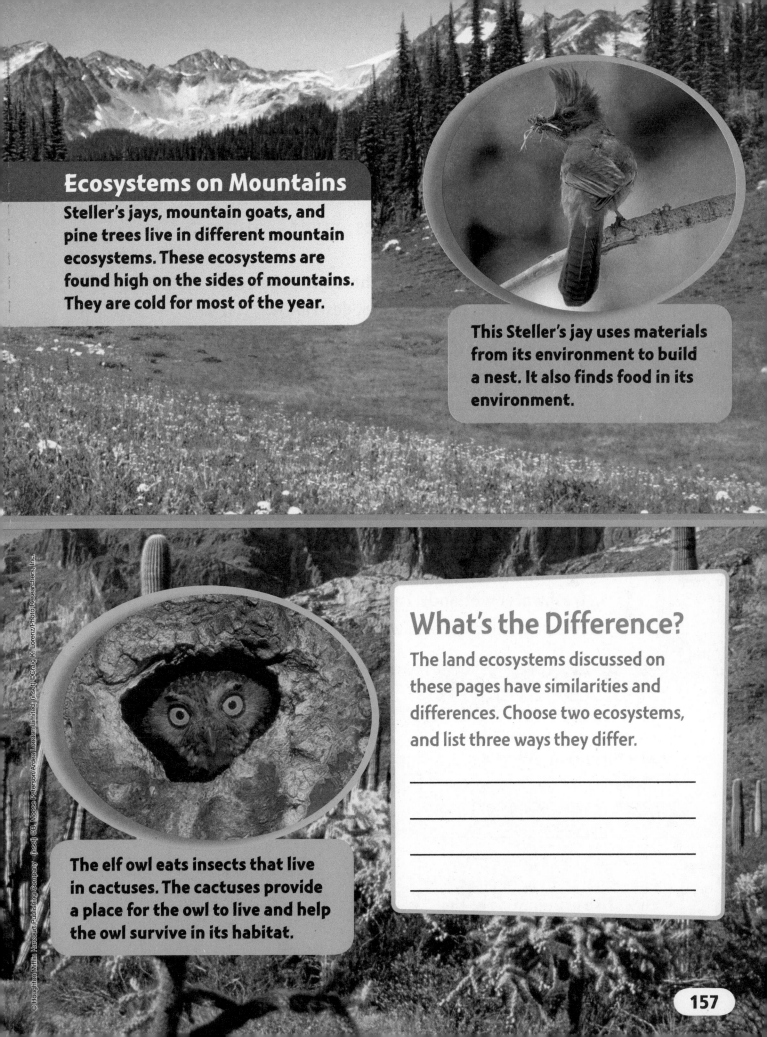

Ecosystems on Mountains

Steller's jays, mountain goats, and pine trees live in different mountain ecosystems. These ecosystems are found high on the sides of mountains. They are cold for most of the year.

This Steller's jay uses materials from its environment to build a nest. It also finds food in its environment.

The elf owl eats insects that live in cactuses. The cactuses provide a place for the owl to live and help the owl survive in its habitat.

What's the Difference?

The land ecosystems discussed on these pages have similarities and differences. Choose two ecosystems, and list three ways they differ.

_____

_____

_____

_____

Under the Water

Most of Earth is covered with water. There are many different living things below the surface of ponds, lakes, rivers, and oceans.

Active Reading As you read these two pages, draw a line from the picture to the sentences that describe it.

If you look at a globe, you'll notice a lot of blue! That blue represents Earth's oceans. The oceans consist of salt water. Animals like sea turtles, whales, and lobsters live in ocean ecosystems. Some ocean animals, like coral, don't look like animals at all. The ocean also has plantlike life forms such as kelp and seaweed.

Rivers, lakes, ponds, and streams are usually fresh water. Fresh water has much less salt than ocean water. Frogs, ducks, and many kinds of fish live in fresh water. Alligators are found in freshwater wetlands. Land animals like deer, foxes, and raccoons drink this fresh water.

Ocean Ecosystem

This huge underwater ecosystem is made by tiny ocean animals called corals.

Clownfish live around sea anemones in their habitat. The clownfish are immune to the anemone's stings, but animals that might eat the clownfish are not!

River Ecosystem

Rivers carry water to the ocean. This flowing water is an ecosystem made of fresh water.

River otters build their shelters next to rivers where they swim and catch fish.

Using the Environment

Describe how the animals in the two photographs use the resources in their environment.

_____

_____

Sum It Up!

When you're done, use the answer key to check and revise your work.

Read each statement. Draw a line to match each statement with the picture it describes.

1 This saltwater ecosystem covers much of the earth's surface.

2 This ecosystem's main plant is grass.

3 This ecosystem has the cactus, a plant that stores water in its stem.

4 Steller's jays and mountain goats live in this ecosystem.

5 Fox and deer drink the fresh water from this water ecosystem.

Desert

Ocean

River

Mountain

Grassland

160

Answer Key: 1–Ocean 2–Grassland 3–Desert 4–Mountain 5–River

Name _____

Word Play

1 Use the clues to help unscramble each word. Write the unscrambled word in the boxes.

1. NOACE

This ecosystem contains salt water.

☐☐☐☐☐

2. SLSADNAGR

Bison and antelope roam this flat ecosystem.

☐☐☐☐☐☐☐☐☐

3. SMCEYOTSE

The living and nonliving things that interact in the same area.

☐☐☐☐☐☐☐☐☐

4. TBHTAAI

Where a plant or an animal lives.

☐☐☐☐☐☐☐

5. NDPO

Cattails and water lilies live near or on this freshwater ecosystem.

☐☐☐☐

6. TMVEINNRONE

The living and nonliving things that surround a living thing.

☐☐☐☐☐☐☐☐☐☐☐

7. YOMCNTUMI

The populations that live in one place.

☐☐☐☐☐☐☐☐☐

8. RTSEDE

Plants and animals that can survive with little water live in this ecosystem.

☐☐☐☐☐☐

9. OLTOPNPUAI

All of one type of organism in the same place.

☐☐☐☐☐☐☐☐☐☐

10. SATRORFENI

Jaguars, toucans, and monkeys live in this ecosystem.

☐☐☐☐☐☐☐☐☐☐

Apply Concepts

2 In what kind of ecosystem would you find these living things?
Write the name of the area underneath each one.

Clownfish

_____

Alligator

_____

Fish

_____

Zebra

_____

Cactus

_____

Toucan

_____

3 Explain the difference between a population and a community.
Give an example of each.

_____

_____

_____

_____

_____

Take It Home!

Go outside and look at the environment around you. What
living things are in your environment? What nonliving things
are in your environment? Record your observations.

Name _____

Essential Question

What's in an Ecosystem?

Set a Purpose
What will you discover in this activity?

_____

_____

_____

Think About the Procedure
Why do you think you will look at the environment inside the coat hanger instead of looking at a larger area?

_____

_____

_____

What living things do you expect to find in your environment?

_____

_____

What nonliving things do you expect to find in your environment?

_____

_____

Record Your Data

Fill in the table with the living and nonliving things you observed in the environment. Estimate items that are too many to count, such as grass.

Living Things	Number	Nonliving Things	Number

Draw Conclusions

How did the wire hanger help you?

_____

_____

_____

_____

What did you learn about the larger ecosystem by studying a small part of it? Explain.

_____

_____

_____

_____

Analyze and Extend

1. What did you find out when you compared your observations with the observations of a classmate? What were some similarities? What were some differences?

_____

_____

_____

_____

_____

2. What did you observe about how the parts of the environment interacted?

_____

_____

_____

_____

3. How have people affected the environment you observed?

_____

_____

_____

4. What are some other questions you have about ecosystems around you?

_____

_____

_____

_____

_____

Meet the Ecosystems Scientists

Dení Ramírez

Dení Ramírez is a marine biologist. She studies the world's largest fish—the whale shark. She spends most of her time in the waters of Mexico. After taking pictures of each shark, she tags them to track their movement. She records where they eat, migrate, and reproduce. Her work helps people understand and protect whale sharks and their habitat.

Each whale shark has a different pattern of spots on its back. Ramírez uses these spots to identify the whale sharks.

Cassandra Nichols

Cassandra Nichols is a scientist who studies climate change. She and a team of scientists study the rain forest in Australia. To reach the top of the rain-forest trees, Nichols uses a very tall crane. Other scientists on the team study the soil, insects, birds, and other animals in the rain forest. Nichols and her team hope to learn how changes in climate affect this ecosystem.

A special tool called a porometer is used to study the leaves of the rain forest.

Know Your Ecosystem!

Label each clue with the letter of the matching picture.

1. These animals live in an ocean ecosystem. _____

2. A rain-forest ecosystem has many nonliving things on the forest floor such as this. _____

3. This is the very top of the rain-forest ecosystem. _____

4. This type of animal is found in the rain forest. _____

5. Most of an ocean ecosystem is made up of this. _____

6. This strange-looking organism lives in the ocean. _____

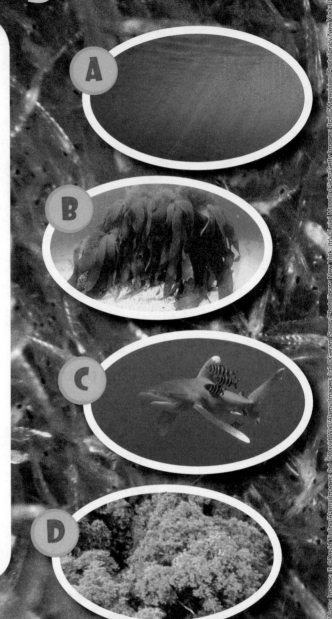

A

B

C

D

E

F

Essential Question

What Is a Food Chain?

Engage Your Brain!

Find the answer to the following question in this lesson and record it here.

What do these two animals and the grasses have in common?

_____

_____

_____

Active Reading

Lesson Vocabulary

List the terms. As you read, make notes about them in the Interactive Glossary.

_____ _____

_____ _____

_____

Sequence

Many ideas in this lesson are connected by a sequence, or order, that describes the steps in a process. Active readers stay focused on sequence when they mark the transition from one step in a process to another.

Soak Up the Sun

Plants need energy to grow and reproduce. Where do you think this energy comes from?

Active Reading As you read these pages, draw one line under the source of energy for producers. Draw two lines under the products of photosynthesis that contain energy.

You eat food, such as tomatoes, to get energy. But all green plants, like these tomato plants, must produce, or make, their own food. A **producer** is a living thing that makes its own food.

The process a plant uses to make food is called **photosynthesis** [foht•oh•SIHN•thuh•sis]. During photosynthesis, plants use the energy from sunlight to change water and carbon dioxide [dy•AHKS•yd], a gas in the air, into sugars. A plant uses the sugars as food for growth, or it stores them. During photosynthesis, plants give off oxygen, a gas that both animals and plants need.

sunlight

Photosynthesis happens in leaves. The sun's energy is used to make sugars, which the plant uses or stores.

© Houghton Mifflin Harcourt Publishing Company • (bkgd) placemat) ©Artville/Getty Images; (br) ©Peter Anderson/Getty Images; (t) ©Enigma/Alamy

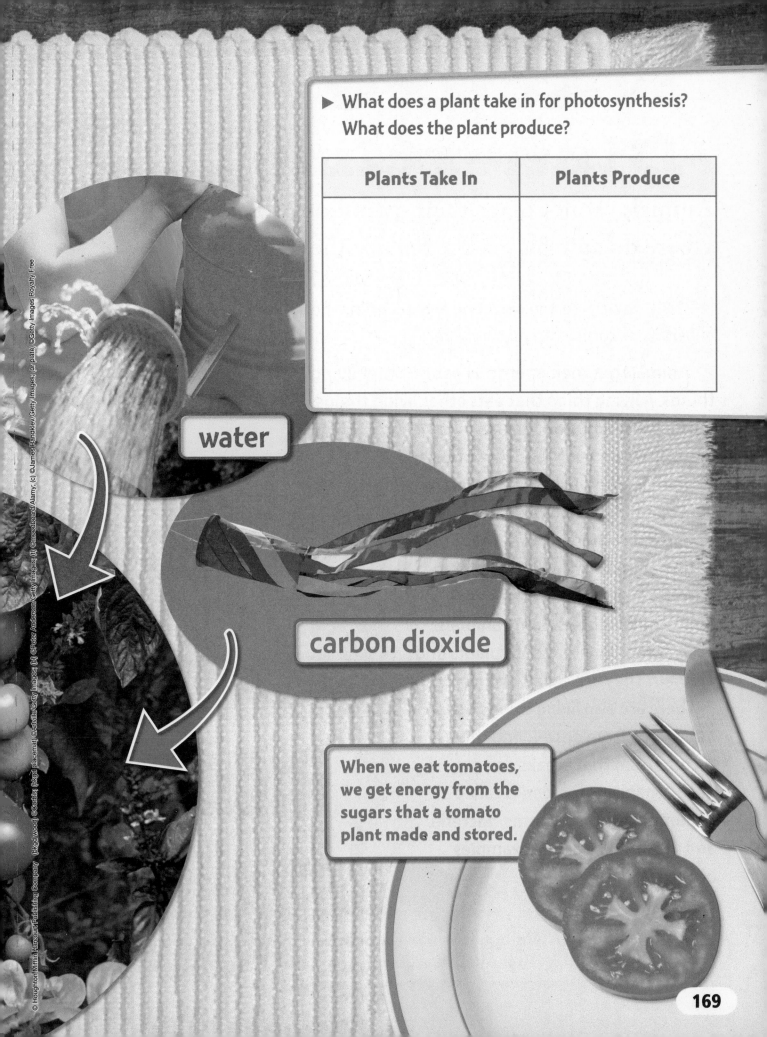

▶ What does a plant take in for photosynthesis? What does the plant produce?

Plants Take In	Plants Produce

water

carbon dioxide

When we eat tomatoes, we get energy from the sugars that a tomato plant made and stored.

Nature's Dinnertime

Animals cannot make their own food. So where do animals get the energy they need?

Active Reading As you read, find and underline the definitions of *herbivore, carnivore,* and *omnivore.*

Animals get their energy by eating other living things. A living thing that eats other living things is called a **consumer**. When a rabbit eats grass, it gets energy from the grass. A rabbit is a *herbivore*, an animal that only eats plants. Some animals get energy by eating only other animals. These meat-eating animals are called *carnivores*. A wolf is a carnivore because it eats animals like rabbits. Some animals, such as raccoons, eat both plants and animals. They are called *omnivores*.

There are also living things that get energy from once-living things. An organism that breaks down dead organisms for food is called a **decomposer**. Earthworms, bacteria, and mushrooms are all examples of decomposers.

A giraffe's neck is long so it can reach the high leaves on trees.

A loggerhead sea turtle eats seaweed and animals like squid and scallops.

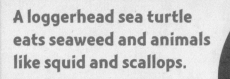

Many decomposers have special chemicals that help them break down dead organisms.

Which Is It?

Decide whether each organism is a carnivore, an omnivore, a herbivore, or a decomposer. Put a check mark in the correct column.

	Carnivore	Omnivore	Herbivore	Decomposer
Sea Turtle				
Jaguar				
Giraffe				
Mushroom				

Jaguars will eat deer, turtles, monkeys, and birds.

Mesquite trees use energy from the sun to produce sugars. They store some of the sugars in their seeds.

Food Chains

A rabbit eats grass. Later, a wolf eats the rabbit. Energy moves from producers, like grass, to consumers, like rabbits and wolves.

Active Reading As you read these two pages, write numbers next to the pictures to show the correct order of events in a food chain.

Energy moves between living things in an ecosystem. A **food chain** shows the path of food from one living thing to another. Grass, rabbits, and wolves are part of a food chain. The rabbits eat the grass, and the wolves eat the rabbits. Energy moves from the sun to the grass to the rabbit to the wolf.

In a food chain, many animals eat other animals. An animal that hunts other animals for food is a *predator*. An animal that is hunted for food is called *prey*. A shark hunts and eats fish in a food chain. The shark is a predator. The fish are the prey. Animals can be both predators and prey in a food chain. Prey for one animal may be a predator of another animal.

Kangaroo rats get energy by consuming mesquite seeds.

▶ Circle the predators and put an X on the prey.

Rattlesnakes eat kangaroo rats to get energy.

The roadrunner is the consumer at the top of this food chain. The energy stored in food passes through the food chain to the roadrunner.

What's for Dinner?

You may have had corn on the cob at a picnic. Corn and other plants grown as food are known as crops.

Crops, such as corn, carrots, and cabbage, are grown on farms all over the United States. Crops are food for people. Crops are also food for livestock, such as cows, pigs, and chickens. Livestock are also raised as food for people. Farmers grow grains to feed livestock. The crops grown by farmers are an important part of a food chain.

Corn is a producer.

Chickens are consumers.
They eat corn.

174

Farmers must meet the needs of plants in order for crops to grow. Crops must get plenty of air, sunlight, and water. To get water to the crops, farmers may dig long ditches. Water is pumped through the ditches to the crops. Farmers also might use sprinklers to water crops.

Sprinkler irrigation brings water to this crop of corn.

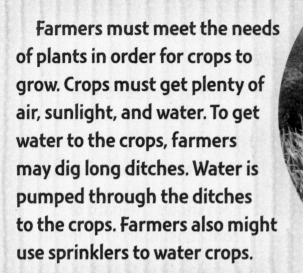

Do the Math!
Solve a Word Problem

It takes 8 pounds of corn to feed 40 chickens each day. How many pounds of corn does it take to feed 40 chickens in one week?

_____

_____

_____

You are a consumer who might eat corn, chicken, or both.

Sum It Up!

When you're done, use the answer key to check and revise your work.

Find and circle the incorrect word in each summary statement. Write the correct word on the line.

1
Plants need carbon dioxide from the air, water, and oxygen to make food.

_____

2
Carnivores eat both plants and animals.

_____

3
Animals that are hunted by other animals are known as predators.

_____

4
A food chain shows the path of energy from consumers to animals.

_____

5
Crops are at the beginning of an important food grain.

_____

© Houghton Mifflin Harcourt Publishing Company (br) ©Justin Guariglia/Corbis

Answer Key: 1. oxygen; sunlight 2. carnivores; omnivores 3. predators; prey 4. consumers; producers 5. grain; chain

Name _____

Word Play

1 Use the clues to complete the crossword puzzle.

Across

1. A living thing that makes its own food

2. The path of food from one living thing to another

6. A living thing that eats other living things

7. An animal that is hunted for food

8. A living thing that breaks down dead organisms for food

Down

1. The process that plants use to make food

3. An animal that eats both plants and animals

4. An animal that hunts other animals for food

5. An animal that eats only plants

6. An animal that eats only other animals

food chain*	producer*	consumer*
herbivore	**carnivore**	**omnivore**
decomposer*	**predator**	**prey**
photosynthesis*		* Key Lesson Vocabulary

Apply Concepts

2 Look at the picture of the food chain below. Label each as either producer or consumer.

_____   _____   _____

3 Label the predator and the prey in each pair of animals.

Shark

_____

Rabbit

_____

Snake

_____

Fish

_____

Wolf

_____

Mouse

_____

4 Think about some foods you eat. Draw a food chain in which you are the last link.

Take It Home!

What crops do you eat? Make a list. Ask members of your family to add to your list. Find out where these crops come from. Are they local, or are they from far away?

Name _____

Essential Question

What Are Some Food Chains?

Set a Purpose
What will you discover in this activity?

_____

_____

_____

_____

What does connecting the cards with yarn and tape show?

_____

_____

_____

_____

Think About the Procedure
Why do you think that the index cards are numbered in the food chain?

_____

_____

_____

_____

_____

_____

Record Your Data
On the lines below, write a description of what happens in your food chain.

_____

_____

_____

_____

_____

_____

Draw Conclusions

How do animals and plants in a food chain depend on each other?

_____

_____

_____

How does the model you made help you to understand food chains?

_____

_____

_____

Analyze and Extend

1. Which animals in the food chain are herbivores? Which animals are carnivores?

_____

_____

_____

2. Which animal is most likely an omnivore? Explain.

_____

_____

_____

_____

3. What do you think would happen if the producer in the food chain was removed from the chain?

_____

_____

_____

_____

4. What do you think would happen if there was a lot of food for the frogs? How would this affect the hawks?

_____

_____

_____

_____

_____

5. What other food chains would you like to learn about?

_____

_____

_____

_____

_____

180

Essential Question

How Do Environmental Changes Affect Living Things?

Engage Your Brain!

Find the answer to the following question in this lesson.

What would the prairie dogs need to do if their habitat was flooded?

_____

_____

_____

Active Reading

Lesson Vocabulary
List the terms. As you read, make notes about them in the Interactive Glossary.

_____ _____

_____

Cause and Effect
Words signaling a cause include *because* and *if*. Words signaling an effect include *so* and *thus*. Active readers remain alert to cause-and-effect signal words.

181

Fragile Ecosystems

In an ecosystem, plants, animals, and other living things share the same environment. But what happens when that environment changes?

Active Reading As you read these two pages, draw a circle around the clue word that signals a cause.

Strong winds have destroyed this forest ecosystem.

In an ecosystem, both living and nonliving things interact. If nonliving things cause the ecosystem to change, the living things will be affected. A powerful storm, for example, may kill plants and animals. Some animals may have to leave to survive. Other animals may stay and have to compete for resources.

Fires cause flame, heat, smoke, and ash. As a result, they can change ecosystems. Fires can be caused by a natural event, like lightning. Fires can also be caused by people. Their effects can be both positive and negative.

NEGATIVE Fires destroy trees and other plants as well as animal habitats.

NEGATIVE This coyote left the fire-burned area to look for a new habitat.

POSITIVE Fires clear space for new plant growth. Ashes from burned plants add nutrients to the soil.

POSITIVE Pinecones open to let their seeds out. Some pinecones will only open when fire heats them.

Write a Headline

Write one headline that describes a positive effect of fire and one headline that describes a negative effect of fire.

_____

_____

The Right Amount of Water

Plants and animals need water to live. But too much or too little water can have a negative effect on an environment.

Active Reading As you read these two pages, find and underline the definitions of *erosion, flood,* and *drought.*

Earth's surface is always wearing down and breaking apart. **Erosion** is when small pieces of rock are carried away by water and sometimes by wind.

When you look at a flowing river, you see more than just moving water. There are also pebbles, sand, and other earth materials. This is erosion. Ocean waves can also cause erosion. Waves hitting a beach carry sand out to sea. As the land wears away, habitats for plants, animals, and people disappear.

Water loosens and moves sand and rock away from the beach. Areas where grass once grew have been washed away by the water.

Erosion is not the only way water affects the environment. Both floods and droughts affect the environment. A **flood** is a large amount of water that covers normally dry land. Floods can happen very suddenly.

A **drought** occurs when it does not rain for a long time. Long droughts force people and animals to look for new places to live. Plants wilt and die.

Finish the Story

Read the start of each story. Look at the photograph. Then finish the story.

Heavy rains this week caused the river to rise higher and higher. Nearby fields were flooded.

We have not had rain in many months. We are now in a drought.

_____

_____

_____

_____

_____

_____

_____

_____

Natural Changes

Water, wind, and other nonliving things can change the environment. But living things can also cause changes.

Active Reading As you read these two pages, draw a star next to what you consider to be the most important sentence, and be ready to explain why.

Animals and plants can make big changes to their environments. Animals can change the environment when they build shelters. Beavers can cause a new lake to form when they build a dam across a river using trees and sticks. The mounds that termites build add nutrients to the soil. The nutrients help plants grow.

Plants can change their environment, too. One kind of plant may take over all the space in an area. This makes it harder for other plants to survive. It can also make it harder for animals to live there.

Some very small living things change environments by causing disease in plants and animals. Diseases harm plants and make animals sick, and can even kill them.

Beavers change the environment when they cut down trees, make canals, and build dams.

Termites can build mounds as high as a three-story building!

Do the Math!

Interpret a Graph

Interpret the line graph. What do you think might have happened to the beech trees in 1999?

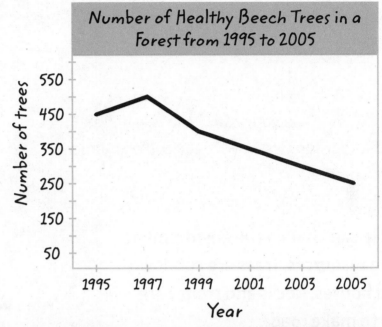

Number of Healthy Beech Trees in a Forest from 1995 to 2005

Number of trees: 50, 150, 250, 350, 450, 550

Year: 1995, 1997, 1999, 2001, 2003, 2005

Some algae blooms release poisons. Algae blooms use up oxygen in the water when the algae die and decompose.

People and the Environment

Can you change the environment? You can and you do! People change the environment every day.

Active Reading As you read these two pages, find and underline two ways that people change the environment.

Reservoirs collect the water that is held back by a dam. People boat, swim, and fish in the reservoir.

People can change the environment by using resources. Trees are cut down to build houses. Rocks and stones are dug up to make roads.

People can change the environment by causing pollution. The exhaust from cars and trucks can pollute the air. Trash can pollute water and land.

People sometimes cause events that usually happen naturally. When people are careless, they can start wildfires. Habitats can be lost when people build dams. In some places, new dams can even cause floods.

People build large dams to control the flow of water. The flow of water is controlled so cities and towns receive just the right amount.

Write an Effect

For each cause, write an effect.

Campers forget to put out their campfire.

_____

_____

Workers build a new road through the forest.

_____

_____

Garbage trucks collect people's trash.

_____

_____

How Can We Help?

Ecosystems change over time. Some changes are natural. Some changes are caused by people. How can people affect the environment in positive ways?

Adding plants to sand dunes can help prevent erosion.

There are many things we can do to help the environment. Turning off a dripping faucet helps conserve water. Turning off lights you are not using helps save energy. If we use less energy, we need fewer resources from the environment.

We can also clean up the environment by cleaning up pollution. We can make smart choices to reduce the amount of trash we throw away. What can you do to help?

Helpful or Not Helpful?

Circle *yes* if the activity helps the environment and *no* if it does not.

polluting the water

yes　　　　　no

cleaning up litter

yes　　　　　no

recycling

yes　　　　　no

bicycling

yes　　　　　no

polluting the air

yes　　　　　no

planting trees

yes　　　　　no

Sum It Up!

When you're done, use the answer key to check and revise your work.

The table below summarizes this lesson. Complete the table.

Environmental Changes Affect Living Things	
People Affect Living Things	**Natural Events Affect Living Things**
1. People can cause natural events like _____.	4. Fire forces animals to leave, but it also makes space for _____.
2. People can cause _____ of air, water, and land habitats.	5. Plants and animals are made sick by _____.
3. One way people can help plants and animals survive is to _____.	6. A beaver building a dam is an example of how animals affect the _____.
	7. Natural events caused by water or lack of it include _____, _____, and _____.

Name _____

Word Play

1 Fill in the missing letters in each word. You will use each of the letters in the box.

| A | B | E | F | G | I | I |
| N | O | O | R | R | S | T |

1. ___ R O ___ I O ___
2. D ___ ___ U ___ H ___
3. H A ___ ___ T ___ T
4. ___ L ___ O D
5. F ___ ___ E

Fill in the blanks with the correct word from above.

6. When rising water causes a _____, animals have to move to dry land.

7. Shorelines and beaches are worn away by _____.

8. A change in the environment can cause an animal to lose its _____.

9. One positive effect of _____ is that some pinecones only open after being heated.

10. When there is not enough rain, _____ can hurt crops.

Apply Concepts

2 Write the missing cause or effect for each picture.

Cause: flood

Effect: _____

Cause: wildfire

Effect: _____

Cause: drought

Effect: _____

Cause: trash

Effect: _____

Cause: one plant uses too many resources

Effect: _____

Cause: _____

Effect: land is flooded

3 Write three ways you could help protect a beach habitat.

_____

_____

Take It Home!

Share what you have learned about environments with your family. Talk about how you can change the environment in positive ways.

Firefighting Tools:
Controlling Forest Fires

Fires play an important role in many forest ecosystems. But large forest fires can damage habitats and homes. Firefighters use special tools to help control forest fires.

Tools like the Pulaski help clear trees and brush. This creates a *firebreak*. Firebreaks stop fires from moving into certain areas.

Some tools protect firefighters. This coat is made from material resistant to fire.

This GPS (Global Positioning System) tool gets information from satellites. It tells firefighters the location of fires.

Special aircraft dump water or chemicals that stop fires.

How can tools help firefighters protect an important habitat?

_____

_____

_____

Solve a Problem

Firefighters need tools to help them stay safe. Other people need safety tools, too. Think of a tool that can help people stay safe. Draw the tool. Tell how it works.

A shovel helps clear underbrush.

How does your tool help people stay safe?

_____

_____

_____

Build On It!

Rise to the engineering design challenge—complete **Design It: Draw a Safari Backpack** on the Inquiry Flipchart.

Name _____

Vocabulary Review

Use the terms in the box to complete the sentences.

consumer
environment
food chain
habitat
producer

1. The place in a forest where a bear lives is called its

   _____.

2. Everything that surrounds a living thing is its

   _____.

3. Because an oak tree can make it own food, it is a(n)

   _____.

4. Producers and consumers are connected in a(n)

   _____.

5. A deer eats other living things, so it is a(n)

   _____.

Science Concepts

Fill in the letter of the choice that best answers the question.

6. Soojinn visited a pond near her house and drew the sketch below. It includes ducks, two kinds of fish, and two kinds of plants.

   How many different populations can be seen in this habitat?

   Ⓐ one

   Ⓑ two

   Ⓒ three

   Ⓓ five

7. Krystina draws a sketch of a desert in her notebook. She includes lizards, cacti, spiders, owls, rocks, and soil. Which would make the best title for Krystina's sketch?

   Ⓐ A Desert Community

   Ⓑ A Desert Ecosystem

   Ⓒ A Desert Population

   Ⓓ A Desert Habitat

Science Concepts

Fill in the letter of the choice that best answers the question.

8. Pablo is studying how animals and plants depend on each other. He set up a terrarium like the one shown here.

What would be most likely to happen if he removed all of the plants from the terrarium?

Ⓐ The insects would reproduce faster.

Ⓑ The insect population would stay the same.

Ⓒ The insects would not get enough food to eat and would die.

Ⓓ The insects would grow bigger because there would be more room in the tank.

9. The weather report says that some parts of the country should expect heavy rainfall for the next two weeks. How might this affect the environment?

Ⓐ A drought will speed up the process of erosion.

Ⓑ A drought will cause some of the plants to die.

Ⓒ Flooding will provide shelter to more animals.

Ⓓ Flooding will cause some animals to have to move away.

10. Mei wants to start a vegetable garden in her yard. While she was choosing a location, a neighbor told her to check the soil for earthworms before she started planting. Why would the neighbor suggest this?

Ⓐ Earthworms cause disease and could harm the plants.

Ⓑ Earthworms are producers and give nutrients to the garden plants.

Ⓒ Earthworms are consumers and will eat the seeds before they can sprout.

Ⓓ Earthworms are decomposers and add nutrients to the soil by breaking down dead organisms.

11. Animals live in a certain habitat depending on their traits and how they live. Look at the picture below.

In which habitat do you think this animal lives?

Ⓐ a desert

Ⓑ a grassland

Ⓒ a rainforest

Ⓓ a river

12. Court goes to the beach for vacation. He takes a picture that looks like the one below.

What conclusion can he make about what is happening to this beach?

(A) Water is eroding it.

(B) Water is soaking it.

(C) Wind is eroding it.

(D) Wind is drying it.

13. Ecosystems are made up of different parts that are related. Which statement below best tells how plants and animals are related?

(A) Plants give off carbon dioxide that animals breathe in.

(B) Plants give off oxygen that animals breathe in.

(C) Plants decompose the dead bodies of animals.

(D) Plants take in air and give off water for animals.

14. Anthony is making a model of a food chain. He wants to show how energy travels through a food chain. Which sequence correctly shows how energy moves among these four organisms?

(A) grass —> rabbit —> fox —> jaguar

(B) grass —> fox —> rabbit —> jaguar

(C) jaguar —> grass —> rabbit —> fox

(D) fox —> jaguar —> grass —>rabbit

15. Shante is starting an environmental club at her school. Which of the activities listed below is a direct way that students can reduce air pollution?

(A) carpool with friends or walk to school

(B) recycle cans and bottles

(C) leave lights on during the day

(D) use plastic bags instead of paper bags

16. A scientist studies a group of zebras that all live together in the same area. She records information about when they migrate. What part of an ecosystem is the scientist studying?

(A) community

(B) environment

(C) habitat

(D) population

Apply Inquiry and Review the Big Idea

Write the answers to these questions.

17. David is investigating the ecosystem in his backyard. The picture below shows his house and yard.

What are the living and nonliving parts of this ecosystem?

a. living

_____

_____

b. nonliving

_____

Which parts of the picture would be part of a community?

_____

_____

18. Maria wondered how different amounts of light given to a plant would affect its growth. Use the space below to describe an investigation she could use to find out.

_____

_____

_____

Name the variable in this experiment.

_____

19. Different populations depend on each other for survival. Explain two ways the bullhorn acacia tree and the ant depend on each other.

a. _____

b. _____

Changes to Earth's Surface

Big Idea

Processes on Earth can change Earth's landforms. Some of these changes happen slowly, while others happen quickly.

Niagara Falls in Canada

I Wonder Why

The edge of Niagara Falls moves back about 30 centimeters every year. Why does this happen? *Turn the page to find out.*

Here's why The force of the flowing water, freezing and thawing, and gravity are causing weathering and erosion of the edge of the falls.

In this unit, you will explore the Big Idea, the Essential Questions, and the Investigations on the Inquiry Flipchart.

Levels of Inquiry Key ■ DIRECTED ■ GUIDED ■ INDEPENDENT

Track Your Progress

Big Idea Processes on Earth can change Earth's landforms. Some of these changes happen slowly, while others happen quickly.

Essential Questions

Now I Get the Big Idea!

Science Notebook

Before you begin each lesson, be sure to write your thoughts about the Essential Question.

Essential Question

What Are Some Landforms?

Find the answer to the following question in this lesson and record it here.

What landform does this river flow through, and how did it form?

_____

_____

_____

Active Reading

Lesson Vocabulary

List the terms. As you learn about each one, make notes in the Interactive Glossary.

_____   _____

_____   _____

_____   _____

Signal Words: Contrasts

Signal words show connections between ideas. Words that signal contrasts include *unlike, different from, but,* and *on the other hand.* Active readers remember what they read because they are alert to signal words that identify contrasts.

Above and Below

Look out the window at the land around you. You might see flat fields, high mountains, a hilly city, or a forest by a lake.

Active Reading As you read this page, circle the definitions of *crust*, *mantle*, *outer core*, and *inner core*.

You can see Earth's surface, but imagine what's under the ground. Earth has several layers.

Crust—The crust is Earth's outer layer. It is made of solid rock.

Mantle—The mantle is the layer below Earth's crust. It is made of soft, hot rock.

Outer Core—Earth's outer core is a layer of liquid metals at Earth's center.

Inner Core—Earth's inner core is a ball of solid metals at Earth's center.

Everything you can see—oceans and land—sits on the crust. The crust is not smooth and flat. If you travel across Earth's surface, you might climb over rolling hills or tall mountains. You might pass through canyons. Each of these is a different landform. A **landform** is a part of Earth's surface that has a certain shape and is formed naturally.

A city may be built on a flat area or on hills or mountains. What landforms are near your home?

Along the coastline, you might find flat areas, hills, or cliffs. What landforms would you travel to see?

True or False

Read each sentence. Circle *True* or *False*.

Earth's center is made of hot, liquid rock.	True	False
There is no crust under the ocean.	True	False
Every landform is part of Earth's crust.	True	False
Mountains and canyons are both landforms.	True	False

Down in the Low Places

When you hike down between hills or mountains, you may end up in a valley. If you look up and see high cliffs, you may have actually walked down into a canyon!

Active Reading As you read these pages, draw boxes around the names of two landforms that are being compared.

A **valley** is the low land between mountains or hills. The sides of valleys are not usually steep. Most valleys are formed by rivers. Some valleys are formed by moving ice.

A **canyon** is a valley with steep sides. Some rivers make canyons as they flow. Over time, soil and loose rock are carried away by the moving water. What is left are tall cliffs that form canyon walls on both sides of the river. The walls of some canyons are very high. The Grand Canyon is about 1,524 meters (5,000 feet) deep from top to bottom!

These people are floating on a river. The river flows between steep canyon walls.

canyon

Over many years, a river may carve out rock to make a steep canyon. The layers of Earth's crust that have been cut through are visible in the cliff walls.

Other rivers flow through gentle valleys. The sides of these valleys are not as steep as the sides of canyons. Valleys are not always formed by rivers, though. Sometimes, a river appears after the valley has formed.

valley

Label the Landforms

Label each landform, using what you know and see.

_____ _____ _____

Climbing High Above

Climbing most hills is easy, if the hill is not too high or steep. Climbing a mountain, however, is another story. The high peaks and jagged edges make it hard to climb!

Mountains are landforms that are much higher than the surrounding land. When two or more pieces of Earth's crust push together, a mountain or mountain range forms. Mountains can also be formed by volcanoes. Some new mountains are growing higher. They are rough and jagged. Older mountains become smaller as they are slowly worn down by wind, water, or ice. As mountains wear down, they also become more rounded. Landforms that are rounded but smaller than mountains are *hills*.

Snow may fall on a cold mountainside even when it's too warm to snow on the hills or plains below.

Mount McKinley, Alaska
6,194 meters (20,320 feet) tall

Monte Mottarone, Italy
1,491 meters (4,890 feet) tall

Hill in Barboursville, Virginia
366 meters (1,200 feet) tall

▶ Draw a line to the part of the scale that is closest to the height of each landform.

6,500 meters

6,000 meters

5,500 meters

5,000 meters

4,500 meters

4,000 meters

3,500 meters

3,000 meters

2,500 meters

2,000 meters

1,500 meters

1,000 meters

500 meters

0 meters

Do the Math!
Estimate the Difference

Estimate to find about how much higher Monte Mottarone is than the hill in Barboursville. Show your work using a number sentence.

_____

Rolling Along the Flats

Traveling across plains is much easier than climbing a mountain. The land is so flat, you can ride a bike across it. Plateaus are flat, too—but you'll have to go up to get to them!

Active Reading As you read, put brackets around clue words that signal when things are being compared or contrasted.

A **plain** is flat land that spreads out over a long distance. Plains are wide open spaces and may form where there used to be seas. Like a plain, a **plateau** is flat. However, a plateau is higher than the land around it. A plateau is typically formed when flat land is pushed high up by the movement of Earth's crust. Plateaus are sometimes found near mountains.

Plains and plateaus are both flat landforms. But a plateau is higher than the land around it. Here you can see that the plateau is much higher than the plain that surrounds it.

210

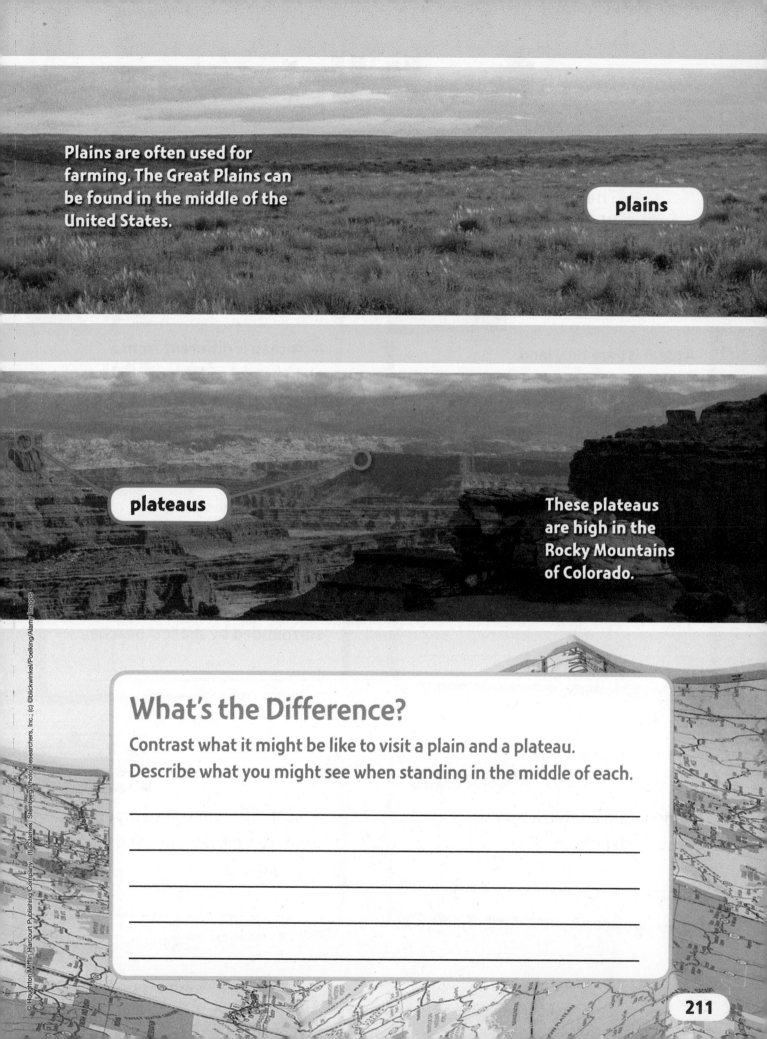

Plains are often used for farming. The Great Plains can be found in the middle of the United States.

plains

plateaus

These plateaus are high in the Rocky Mountains of Colorado.

What's the Difference?

Contrast what it might be like to visit a plain and a plateau. Describe what you might see when standing in the middle of each.

_____

_____

_____

_____

_____

Sum It Up!

When you're done, use the answer key to check and revise your work.

The blue part of each summary statement is incorrect. Write words to replace the blue parts.

1

A plain is very hilly land.

_____

2

A plateau is different from a plain because plateaus are lower than the nearby land.

_____

3

A valley is up high between hills or mountains.

_____

4

A canyon is different from a valley because a canyon is surrounded by shallow beaches.

_____

5

A mountain is often a very short and rounded landform.

_____

6

A hill is different from a mountain because a hill is higher and more jagged.

_____

Answer Key: 1. flat 2. higher 3. down low 4. steep cliffs 5. high and jagged 6. lower and rounder

Name _____

Word Play

1 Fill in the missing letters to find each word. You will use each of the letters in the box.

A	A	A	A	A	A	A	E
E	E	I	I	O	O	O	U	U

1. M __ __ N T __ __ N
2. P L __ T __ __ __ __
3. C __ N Y __ N
4. V __ L L __ Y
5. P L __ __ N
6. L __ N D F __ R M S

Fill in each blank with the correct word from above.

7. A _____ may be thousands of feet high.

8. The cliffs of the _____ towered over the kayakers.

9. The town was sheltered in the deep _____.

10. The flat land was pushed up, leaving a wide _____.

11. Earth's crust is covered with different kinds of _____.

12. A _____ may have once been a sea.

Apply Concepts

2 Draw a picture of the landforms described. Label each landform.

Low place between
mountains

_____

Flat place up high

_____

Place where a river
has carved out cliffs

_____

3 Read the descriptions of Earth's layers. Then complete the labels.
Draw lines to the correct layers.

Liquid metal layer: _____

Solid metal layer: _____

Cool, solid rock: _____

Soft, hot rock: _____

Take It Home!

Make a plan for a walking or hiking trip with your family. Think
of two different landforms you can visit on your trip.

How Does Earth's Surface Change Slowly?

Essential Question

Engage Your Brain!

Find the answer to the following question in this lesson and record it here.

This glacier is moving slowly. How is it affecting the land around it?

_____

_____

_____

Active Reading

Lesson Vocabulary

List the terms. As you read, make notes about them in the Interactive Glossary.

_____   _____

_____

Signal Words: Main Idea

Words that signal a main idea include *most important* and *in general*. Active readers remember what they read because they are alert to signal words that identify important ideas.

What Weathering Can Do

Animals, plants, water, and temperature are just some of the things that can change Earth's surface.

Active Reading As you read these two pages, underline details about what water does to change Earth's surface.

Weathering is the breaking down of rock into smaller pieces. This can happen when tree roots push into the surface of rock. It can happen when animals burrow into the ground.

Weathering is often caused by patterns of freezing and thawing. As winter nears, the weather gets colder. Rain falls into cracks in rock and freezes. As liquid water turns to ice, it expands. This widens the cracks. When the ice melts, or thaws, the rock is weaker. Pieces crumble and fall away. Little by little, the shape of the rock changes. Smaller pieces of rock may become part of the soil.

Change Takes Time

Changing seasons cause patterns of freezing and thawing. This is one way weathering happens.

Water moves into cracks and stays there.

Weathering by water has caused these rocks to become rounded. Freezing water has also caused some of the rocks to crack.

▶ Draw the next stage of weathering for this rock.

1

2

3

The water freezes. Ice forms in the cracks. The ice takes up more space than the liquid water did.

The ice widens the cracks. Pieces of rock may break off.

Erosion Motion

Water, wind, and glaciers never stop moving. They carry soil, rocks, and sand along with them. Over time, this movement changes the shape of the land.

Active Reading As you read, circle a word or a phrase that signals a main idea.

In general, **erosion** happens when soil, rocks, or sand are moved. Wind, water, and glaciers can all cause erosion. It happens everywhere. When waves at a beach wash away sand, that's erosion. When wind blows sand in a desert, that's erosion. When rainfall carries mud into a river, that's erosion.

Glaciers are another cause of erosion. A **glacier** is a large, thick sheet of moving ice. Glaciers slide along slowly. As they move, many glaciers cut paths through the ground. They pick up pieces of weathered rock, sand, and soil. Glaciers push or carry the rocks and soil as they move. Sometimes glaciers move enough soil to form a whole island!

Wind and waves cause weathering as they hit the rock. This breaks the rock into smaller pieces.

Wind and water move sand. This erosion causes one part of the beach to become smaller. Another part of the beach becomes larger when the eroded sand is left there.

Over time, erosion can cause big changes. It has caused this beach to become much smaller than it once was.

When this lighthouse was built, it was far from the cliff's edge. But wind and waves have weathered and eroded the cliff. Now, the lighthouse must be moved to a safer spot.

Do the Math!
Solve a Word Problem

A lighthouse is 60 meters from the edge of a cliff. The cliff erodes by 3 meters each year. How long will it take for the edge of the cliff to reach the lighthouse? Show your work.

_____

Sand, soil, and small rocks erode away. The eroded material moves into the water and away from the land.

Soil Moves Around

Erosion can ruin fields and forests by taking away soil the plants need. But soil that is washed away from one place can help plants in another place.

Active Reading As you read, underline the harmful and helpful effects of erosion.

As a river flows between its banks, soil and rocks are swept along. The water carries them downstream. Now, there is less soil on the riverbanks. Tree roots may be uncovered. Plants that need the soil may be affected. Without the support of their roots anchored in deep soil, the trees may fall.

But soil that is washed away from a riverbank ends up somewhere else. As a river nears the ocean, the water moves more slowly. The rocks and soil in the river are dropped. This process makes a landform called a *delta*. A river delta is full of rich soil.

Water has eroded soil from this riverbank. These trees may soon fall.

The river's motion carries soil downstream. This leaves less soil for the plants that are growing here.

As a river nears the ocean, the water slows. Soil and rocks in the river are left behind.

Over time, the rocks and soil form a delta. The rich soil of a river delta is a great place for plants to grow.

Cause and Effect
Fill in the blanks to tell the causes and effects of erosion.

1. Moving water carries rocks and _____ downstream.

2. Growing _____ along the riverbanks may become loose.

3. Tree _____ may be uncovered, causing the trees to fall.

4. The rocks and soil may be deposited, forming a _____.

Sum It Up!

When you're done, use the answer key to check and revise your work.

Fill in the missing words in the summary. Then complete the cause-and-effect graphic organizer.

Summarize

Weathering and erosion are two processes that (1) _____ the shape of Earth's surface. When large pieces of rock are broken down into smaller pieces, it is called (2) _____. Erosion is when (3) _____, wind, or glaciers carry these smaller rocks to new places. Erosion can change beaches and riverbanks by taking sand and (4) _____ away. But it can also make new landforms, such as river (5) _____.

Cause		Effect
Waves crash against a cliff.	→	6. _____ _____ _____ _____
7. _____ _____ _____ _____	→	A lighthouse needs to be moved.

Name _____

Word Play

1 Use the words in the box at the bottom of the page to complete the puzzle.

Across

2. A river carries soil here
4. To melt after freezing
5. This part of a plant can cause weathering.
8. When wind and water move rocks, sand, or soil
9. A large, moving sheet of ice
10. When a solid turns to a liquid

Down

1. Breaking of rock into smaller pieces
3. Another word for stones
6. Change from a liquid to a solid
7. When this is washed away, plants cannot grow.

rocks	delta
thaw	weathering*
glacier*	root
melt	erosion*
soil	freeze

* Key Lesson Vocabulary

Apply Concepts

2 For each picture, draw how the object in the picture would change.

 **+** time **+** waves **=**

 **+** time **+** rain **=**

 **+** time **+** rushing river **=**

3 Name two things that can happen when soil is eroded by a river.

_____

_____

_____

Take It Home!

With your family, talk about weathering and erosion. Identify something in your neighborhood that has changed over time because of these processes.

Sand and Surf:
Erosion Technology

There is often more than one solution to an engineering problem. To choose the best solution, people make trade-offs. A trade-off is giving up one feature to make another feature better. Read about the trade-offs of two beach erosion solutions.

People can control beach erosion by building a jetty. A jetty begins on a beach and runs into the water. It is at a right angle to the shore.

Jetty Pluses	Jetty Minuses
Easier to build above water	Erodes beach on other side of jetty
Can be built quickly	Changes the natural look of the beach

People can control beach erosion by building a reef. A reef is under water. It runs in the same direction as the shore.

Reef Pluses	Reef Minuses
Does not erode nearby beaches	Harder to build under water
Lowers wave energy before it reaches beach	Takes time for the reef to form

S.T.E.M.
continued

Analyze Trade-offs

Below are two solutions for soil erosion. Fill in the charts to show the trade-offs. Then tell which you would choose and why.

Hay Bales Pluses	Hay Bales Minuses

Silt Fence Pluses	Silt Fence Minuses

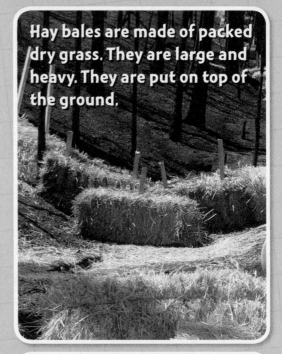

Hay bales are made of packed dry grass. They are large and heavy. They are put on top of the ground.

A silt fence is made of lightweight plastic. The bottom is dug into the ground.

Which soil erosion solution would you choose? Why?

_____

_____

Build On It!

Rise to the engineering design challenge—complete **Improvise It: Reducing Erosion** on the Inquiry Flipchart.

© Houghton Mifflin Harcourt Publishing Company (t) ©Kevin Moloney/Getty Images; (b) ©Kim Karpeles/Alamy Images

DESIGN PROCESS STEPS

Name _____

Essential Question

How Can We Model Erosion?

Set a Purpose
What will you learn from this modeling activity?

_____

_____

Think About the Procedure
What does the sand represent? What does the ice cube represent?

_____

_____

_____

Why will you push the ice over clay before you push it over the sand and clay?

_____

_____

_____

Record Your Observations
Use words or drawings to show how the ice and sand interact.

	Sight	Touch
Clay Without Sand		
Clay With Sand		

Draw Conclusions

How does a glacier affect the land it moves over?

_____

_____

_____

_____

Analyze and Extend

1. What force causes a glacier to move downhill?

_____

_____

_____

2. You pushed the ice over the clay and soil to see the effects of a glacier. In nature, glaciers travel much more slowly. How could you model the way that glaciers move in nature?

_____

_____

_____

_____

3. As glaciers move down a slope to the sea, do they cause weathering, erosion, or both? Explain your answer.

_____

_____

_____

_____

_____

_____

_____

4. What are some other questions you have about glaciers and how glaciers affect the land?

_____

_____

_____

_____

_____

_____

Essential Question

How Does Earth's Surface Change Quickly?

Engage Your Brain!

Find the answer to the following question in this lesson and record it here.

These used to be living plants, but now they are dead. The ground is covered in ash. What might have caused these changes?

_____

_____

Active Reading

Lesson Vocabulary

List the terms. As you learn about each one, make notes in the Interactive Glossary.

_____

_____

_____

Signal Words: Sequence

Signal words show connections between ideas. Words that signal sequence include *now, before, after, first, next,* and *then.* Active readers remember what they read because they are alert to signal words that identify sequence.

Earthquake!
Shaken Up

Earth's surface begins to shake. The ground splits. Buildings crack, and some fall. What's happening?

Active Reading As you read this page, underline the clue word that signals a cause.

An **earthquake** is a shaking of Earth's surface that can cause land to rise and fall. Most earthquakes are too weak to be felt, but strong earthquakes can cause a big change to Earth's surface. What causes earthquakes?

Earthquakes happen because of movements in Earth's crust. They occur mostly in places where two pieces of crust meet. Pieces may push together, pull apart, or slide past each other. The map shows places where earthquakes are most likely to happen.

An earthquake can cause great damage over a small or large area.

► The legend next to the map shows an area's risk for earthquakes. Use the legend to answer the questions below the map.

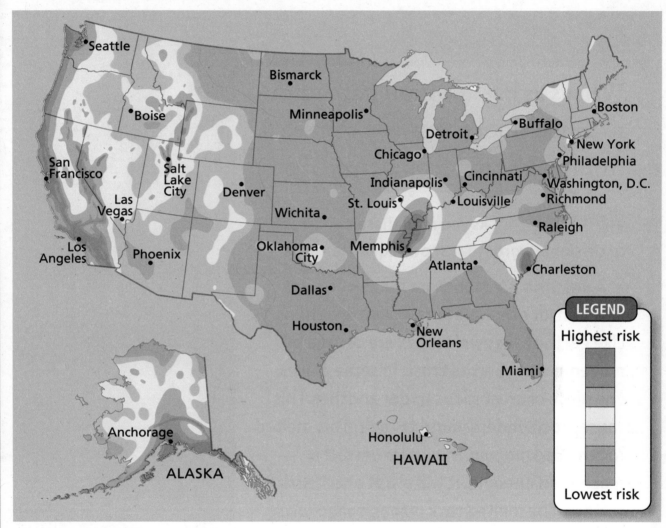

Does San Francisco or Boise have the highest earthquake risk?

_____

Find Dallas and Miami on the map. Which city has the lowest earthquake risk?

_____

Volcano!
Feel the Heat

What's as big as a mountain with so much smoke that you can see it from space? Read on to find out!

Active Reading As you read these two pages, circle signal words that show sequence.

A **volcano** is a mountain made of cooled lava, ash, or other materials from eruptions. Like earthquakes, volcanoes are caused by movements of Earth's crust. In some places, one piece of crust slides under another. This causes rock underground to melt. This melted rock, called *magma*, moves upward. If it reaches an opening, it will erupt onto Earth's surface. The melted rock is then called *lava*. As the lava cools, it gets hard. Some volcanoes grow larger with every eruption.

In some volcanoes, lava gently oozes out. Other volcanoes explode! Lava, stone, and ash are thrown from the volcano's opening with tremendous force. Exploding volcanoes can quickly change Earth's surface.

Red-hot melted rock called magma comes up from underground. When it reaches the surface, we call it lava.

In May 1980, Mount St. Helens erupted. First, there was an earthquake. Then, the volcano began to spit out lava and ash. The eruption went on for nine hours. Nearly 379 square kilometers (230 square miles) of forest was buried or blown down.

Before it erupted, Mount St. Helens, in Washington State, was 2,950 meters (9,677 feet) high. Many plants and animals lived on the mountain.

The eruption of Mount St. Helens sent more than one trillion pounds of ash across the United States. Many plants and animals that lived on the mountain died.

Years later, the mountain is more than 305 meters (1,000 feet) lower, but life has returned. The mountain again provides habitats for many different plants and animals.

What Happened Here?

Look at the images above. Describe how Mount St. Helens has changed the land around it.

_____

_____

_____

Big Changes
Fire, Water, Mud

A little bit of fire, water, or dirt can be very useful. But what if there is too much?

Active Reading As you read, underline the main idea about each big change. Circle details that tell more about each idea.

A forest fire starts small. It can be sparked by lightning, a bit of lava, or a careless person. People have to act quickly to control forest fires.

Too much rain in too short a period of time can cause a flood. A **flood** is a change that happens when streams, rivers, or lakes get too full and overflow. Entire towns can be destroyed. Many plants may die, and animals may have to find new homes. Over time, floodwater drains away, dries up, or is absorbed into the ground.

Floodwaters in Nashville, Tennessee

Sometimes, water from rain or a flood loosens dirt on the side of a hill or mountain. The dirt slides downhill in a mudslide or landslide. It may bury part of a town.

Do the Math!

Skip Count by 5s

The Smith River overflows its banks after at least 30 centimeters of rainfall in one day. Rain is falling at 5 centimeters an hour. How long will it have to rain before the river overflows?

_____

Be Prepared
Planning Ahead

How do you prepare for a disaster? You make an emergency plan and prepare your home. You make sure any pets will be safe, too!

People do many things to prepare for disasters. Buildings are designed to withstand earthquakes. The sides of rivers are built up to prevent floods. News reports let us know about the risk of forest fires. Radio, television, and the Internet warn us about storms and other emergencies.

Emergency plans can help keep us safe. Families can talk about what to do in an emergency. A list like the one on the next page can help.

It's best to prepare for a disaster before it strikes. Keeping supplies in your car can help you be ready.

First Aid Kit

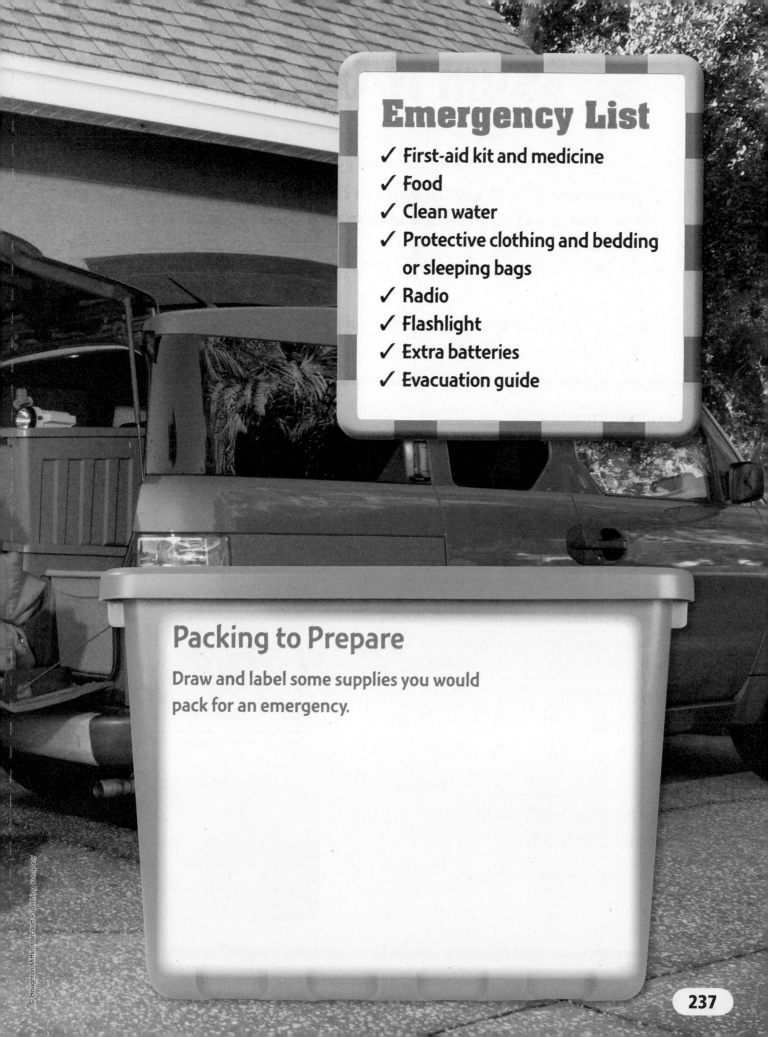

Emergency List

✓ First-aid kit and medicine
✓ Food
✓ Clean water
✓ Protective clothing and bedding or sleeping bags
✓ Radio
✓ Flashlight
✓ Extra batteries
✓ Evacuation guide

Packing to Prepare

Draw and label some supplies you would pack for an emergency.

Sum It Up!

When you're done, use the answer key
to check and revise your work.

**Use the words in the word bank to complete each group
of sentences. Then draw a line to match the sentences with
a picture.**

> drain   ground   water   lava   ash   volcano   flood   earthquake

1 During storms, _____
may overflow a river or lake. This is
called a(n) _____.
The water may _____
away or dry up later.

2 Melted rock called _____
explodes onto Earth's surface,
and _____
fills the sky. A(n) _____
has erupted.

3 The _____ shakes
when pieces of Earth's crust push
together. This is called
a(n) _____.

Name _____

Word Play

1 Use the words in the box to complete the puzzle.

Down

1. Movements in Earth's _____ can cause earthquakes.

3. Melted rock beneath Earth's surface is called _____.

5. Too much rain can cause a _____.

7. Melted rock that flows onto Earth's surface is _____.

Across

2. Lightning can cause a _____ _____.

4. An _____ can cause buildings to fall over.

6. When a lot of wet soil moves down a hillside, it is called a _____.

8. When a _____ erupts, it can cause a lot of damage.

flood*   earthquake*

forest fire   mudslide

volcano*   lava

magma   crust

* Key Lesson Vocabulary

Apply Concepts

2 Describe how the named events might affect the environments shown.

Flood	_____ _____ _____ _____	_____ _____ _____ _____
Earthquake	_____ _____ _____ _____	_____ _____ _____ _____
Forest fire	_____ _____ _____ _____	_____ _____ _____ _____

Take It Home!

Talk to your family about types of natural disasters that could occur in your area. Discuss some ways that you can be prepared for these events.

Meet the Earth Scientists

Waverly Person 1927-

Before he retired in 2006, Waverly Person was the director of an earthquake center. When an earthquake struck, Person calculated the size, or magnitude, of it. Then he shared the information about what had happened with news sources. He would also warn the public about any damage. Although he is retired, Person is still one of the experts that people first go to for information about earthquakes.

Special instruments detect earthquakes all over the world. Once detected,

Hugo Delgado Granados 1957-

Hugo Delgado Granados studies the relationship between active volcanoes and Earth's moving crust. He studies the volcano Popocatépetl [poh•puh•KAT•uh•pet'l] in Mexico. Glaciers, or slowly moving masses of ice, cover its top. Granados uses a remote device to measure the gases coming from the volcano. Changes in the ice or gases tell Granados about the volcano's activity.

Glaciers cover the top of Popocatépetl. These glaciers are measured for changes caused by volcanic activity.

Be an Earth Scientist!

A scale like the one at left is used to show an earthquake's magnitude. The strength of volcanic eruptions is measured using the scale at right. Use the scales to answer the questions.

On this scale, the higher numbers mean stronger earthquakes.

Earthquake Magnitude Scale (1–8)

10	Extraordinary
9	Outstanding
8	Far-reaching
7	High
6	Noteworthy
5	Intermediate
4	Moderate
3	Minor
2	Low
1	Insignificant

On this scale, the higher numbers mean stronger volcanic eruptions.

Volcanic Explosivity Index (0–8)

VEI	Description
0	non-explosive
1	gentle
2	explosive
3	severe
4	cataclysmic
5	paroxysmal
6	colossal
7	super-colossal
8	mega-colossal

1 An earthquake has occurred that is a 1 on the scale. Why won't emergency crews be needed? _____

2 A far-reaching earthquake measures _____ on the scale.

3 Which volcano eruption is stronger: colossal or severe? _____

4 What does an explosive eruption measure on the volcanic scale? _____

Mifflin Harcourt Publishing Company   (bg) ©needboard RF/Photolibrary/New York

Unit 5 Review

Name _____

Vocabulary Review

Use the terms in the box to complete the sentences.

> canyon
> erosion
> mountain
> volcano
> weathering

1. When two or more pieces of Earth's crust push together, they form a(n) _____.

2. When a river flows over time, it can leave a deep groove with tall sides called a(n) _____.

3. Lava can ooze or erupt from a
   _____.

4. When waves on a beach wash away sand, you will see
   _____.

5. A rock breaks apart after freezing and thawing many times. This is an example of _____.

Science Concepts

Fill in the letter of the choice that best answers the question.

6. How can glaciers cause erosion?

   Ⓐ They can push together Earth's surface, making mountains.

   Ⓑ They can cause vibrations that crack the Earth's crust.

   Ⓒ They can pick up bits of rock and soil and carry them as they move.

   Ⓓ They can fill cracks in rocks that get larger and break the rocks.

7. Earth has different layers. Which is the **best** description for the mantle?

   Ⓐ solid

   Ⓑ thin layer

   Ⓒ hot, soft rock

   Ⓓ dense rock and metal

Science Concepts

Fill in the letter of the choice that best answers the question.

8. Which of these is a sudden change in Earth's surface that can be harmful to living things?

   Ⓐ erosion

   Ⓑ a forest fire

   Ⓒ a glacier

   Ⓓ weathering

9. The drawing below shows the movement in two pieces of Earth's crust.

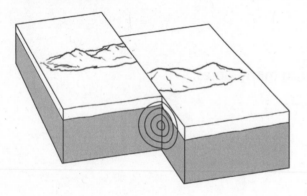

   What does this drawing show?

   Ⓐ an earthquake

   Ⓑ a flood

   Ⓒ a fire

   Ⓓ a volcanic eruption

10. Over many years, a mountain is weathered and eroded. What landform will the mountain gradually change into?

    Ⓐ a canyon

    Ⓑ a hill

    Ⓒ a volcano

    Ⓓ a valley

11. Which describes how water can cause weathering?

    Ⓐ Rivers flow through a canyon. As they move, they carry rocks with them, making the canyon steeper.

    Ⓑ Water flows into cracks in rocks. The water freezes, making the cracks larger and breaking down the rock.

    Ⓒ Glaciers are made of ice. As they move, they pick up pieces of soil and rock and move the soil and rock along with them.

    Ⓓ Rain falls quickly during a storm. This causes the mud on a hill to move and large areas of dirt and rock to slide down a hill.

12. Look at the landform below.

Which **best** describes how it was formed?

Ⓐ One piece of crust slid beneath another. Lava began to push up through the cracks.

Ⓑ Two pieces of crust pushed against each other. As they pushed, they forced part of the crust upward to create this landform.

Ⓒ Two pieces of crust pulled apart, causing vibrations and a large crack to open.

Ⓓ A river brought rocks and dirt to this point. Over time, the dirt and rocks formed layers that built up.

13. Tran's class is visiting a delta to make observations. The students observe rich soil. What is the most likely reason for this?

Ⓐ Rocks in the delta were ground into soil.

Ⓑ The soil was carried into the delta by the wind.

Ⓒ The soil was washed into the delta by a flowing river.

Ⓓ Rocks from the ocean were ground up by ocean waves.

14. Keesha puts some brick pieces, sand, and water in a jar. She shakes it each day for two weeks and notices what happens to the brick pieces and water. What is she modeling?

Ⓐ how a volcano erupts

Ⓑ how weathering forms soil

Ⓒ how floodwater is absorbed

Ⓓ how earthquakes change rocks

15. On which layer of Earth do you find oceans, mountains, and valleys?

Ⓐ crust

Ⓑ inner core

Ⓒ mantle

Ⓓ outer core

Apply Inquiry and Review the Big Idea

Write the answers to these questions.

16. Tomas took a picture of the landform below. He shared it with his class.

Tell which landform is pictured. How is it like a plain? How is it different?

_____

_____

_____

17. Drew went on a campout in the desert. He saw the sand structures below and wondered how they were made naturally.

Explain a likely cause of these sand structures.

_____

_____

_____

18. Sari has a large pan, some dirt, rocks, books, a watering can, and water. How could she use those to show what happens during a landslide?

_____

_____

_____

People and Resources

Big Idea

Living things use Earth's resources to meet their needs. Some of these resources can be recycled or reused.

Hoover Dam, Nevada

I Wonder Why

Why did people build a huge dam like this? What resources are they using? *Turn the page to find out.*

Houghton Mifflin Harcourt Publishing Company

Here's why Dams harness the power of moving water to produce electricity from generators.

In this unit, you will explore the Big Idea, the Essential Questions, and the Investigations on the Inquiry Flipchart.

Levels of Inquiry Key ■ DIRECTED ■ GUIDED ■ INDEPENDENT

Track Your Progress

Big Idea Living things use Earth's resources to meet their needs. Some of these resources can be recycled or reused.

Essential Questions

Now I Get the Big Idea!

Science Notebook

Before you begin each lesson, be sure to write your thoughts about the Essential Question.

Essential Question

What Are Some Natural Resources?

Engage Your Brain!

Find the answer to the following question in this lesson and record it here.

How does this wind farm help people use a natural resource?

_____

_____

_____

Active Reading

Lesson Vocabulary

List the terms. As you learn about each one, make notes in the Interactive Glossary.

_____

_____

_____ _____

_____ _____

Compare and Contrast

Many ideas in this lesson are connected because they explain comparisons and contrasts—how things are alike and different. Active readers stay focused on comparisons and contrasts when they ask themselves, How are these things alike? How are they different?

249

Natural Resources

Most of the things you use every day come from nature. But how do we get these things? How do we use them?

Active Reading As you read, underline the definitions for *natural resource* and *renewable resource*.

A **natural resource** is something that comes from nature that people can use. The air you breathe, and the soil that crops grow in are natural resources. Other natural resources are used to make products you may use. Can you guess which natural resource is used to make paper and pencils?

Paper and pencils are made from trees. Trees are a **renewable resource**—one that can be replaced easily. We can plant more trees to make more paper and pencils.

Wood from a tree was used to make this bat. Even though trees can be replaced, we have to be careful not to use them too quickly. New trees take time to grow.

The food we eat comes from nature. Fish that are caught in the ocean are sold to people in stores and markets.

Fish are a renewable resource. Young fish replace those that are caught. Other animals also eat fish. We have to be careful not to eat fish more quickly than they can be replaced.

Water is an important resource. We drink water and also use it for many other things. We can use falling water to produce energy. If we clean water, we can use it again.

Some natural resources are used to make reusable products. You can use this plastic water bottle over and over again.

What Resources Do You Use?

List three natural resources you see on the page. Choose a resource and describe how you use it.

_____

_____

Going, Going, Gone

Not all natural resources are renewable. Some natural resources will eventually be used up and be gone.

Active Reading As you read, underline the sentence that compares three nonrenewable resources.

Coal is a nonrenewable resource burned to make electricity. Computers, lights, and electric heaters all use electricity.

Many resources are found underground. People dig for copper at this mine. Oil, coal, and natural gas can also be found underground.

© Houghton Mifflin Harcourt Publishing Company (bg) ©William Robinson/Alamy Images;

A **nonrenewable resource** is a natural resource that can be used up. Oil, coal, and natural gas are nonrenewable resources we use to produce different kinds of energy, including electricity. They are **fossil fuels**—fuels that form over many years from the remains of once-living organisms.

How can we make sure these resources don't disappear too quickly? We have to conserve them. **Conservation** is saving resources by using them wisely. What are some ways that you can use nonrenewable resources wisely? You can start by turning off lights when you don't need them.

Gemstones, like this ruby, are taken from the ground. Gemstones are a nonrenewable resource used to make jewelry.

Renewable or Nonrenewable?

Decide whether each resource is renewable or nonrenewable. Put an X in the correct column.

Resource	Renewable	Nonrenewable
Wind	X	
Natural Gas		X
Corn		
Diamond		
Oil		
Water		

How Do We Use It?

Food. Water. Electricity. Gasoline. Everything we use comes from nature somehow.

Active Reading As you read these two pages, underline examples of products that come from natural resources.

An oil rig pumps oil, a fossil fuel, from deep within Earth.

raw copper

copper wire

Have you ever wondered what is inside a computer cord? Copper! Electricity moves very well through this nonrenewable resource.

wood furniture

a wood log

For hundreds of years, people have used wood to make all sorts of products. Wood is used to make paper, some tools, and furniture.

Look around the room. Everything you see comes from natural resources. Books, shelves, desks, toys—they're all made from Earth materials.

Even the materials that make up a computer come from Earth. The outside and the inside of a computer are both made from natural resources. Glass computer screens are made from sand. The plastic parts can be produced from oil. To operate, computers also need electricity from fossil fuels.

We also depend upon renewable resources. Imagine you are standing outside. You feel the sun and the wind. These are two important renewable sources of energy.

Solar cells like the ones in these solar panels turn renewable energy into energy we can use.

a cotton plant

cotton clothing

Many of the clothes we wear are made from natural materials such as cotton. Cotton comes from a plant.

Where Does It Come From?

Trees are used to help build homes. What steps must happen for the wood from trees to be used in homes?

_____

_____

_____

_____

_____

The Effects of Pollution

What's that smell? Pollution can make the air, land, and water smell awful. Some of the ways we use natural resources can be harmful.

Active Reading As you read this page, underline all the causes of pollution.

Smoke from this factory mixes with the air. This makes the air harmful to breathe.

What is pollution? **Pollution** is harmful substances in the environment. Smoke in the air is pollution. So are chemicals in water and garbage on land.

What causes pollution? Pollution often results from people using natural resources. Burning fossil fuels, such as gasoline in cars and coal for energy, can cause air pollution. Land pollution is caused when people don't put trash where it belongs. When chemicals and wastes get into water, they cause water pollution.

What's the Cause?

Write one sentence to show how people caused each type of pollution shown.

Land Pollution

_____

_____

_____

Water Pollution

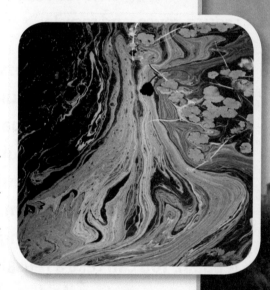

_____

_____

_____

Air Pollution

_____

_____

_____

Reduce, Reuse,

People need natural resources to survive, but we have to use them responsibly. You can help by remembering the "3 Rs"—reduce, reuse, and recycle.

Active Reading As you read this page, underline ways to reduce, reuse, and recycle.

To *reduce* means to use less of something. There are many ways to use fewer natural resources. You can use both sides of a piece of paper, for example. To conserve fossil fuels, you could ride a bike instead of riding in a car. And you could turn off the lights when you leave a room.

When you *reuse* something, you use it again. You can take a reusable bag to the grocery store. And you can use a refillable water bottle.

When you *recycle* something, it is made into a new product. Glass, aluminum cans, paper, plastic bottles, and yard waste can all be recycled. Even the oil from cars can be recycled!

Recycling keeps billions of pounds of material from being thrown in the trash.

WE RECYCLE

Recycle

Glass can be recycled. After glass is recycled, it can be used again.

Crushed glass from the blue bottle is combined with more crushed glass. The glass is then heated. This makes it easy to form into new shapes.

When glass is recycled, it may not be used for the same purpose. Some of the glass in this vase came from the blue bottle.

Do the Math!
Solve a Story Problem

Akeem uses 9 sheets of paper each day. To reduce, he decides to use each sheet of paper 3 times instead of 1 time. How many sheets of paper will he use each day now? _____

Sum It Up!

When you're done, use the answer key to check and revise your work.

Change the circled part of each statement to make it correct.

1

Renewable resources are natural resources that (will run out.)

_____

2

(Gemstone fuels,) such as oil, must be conserved.

_____

3

Coal is a (renewable resource) that can be burned to produce the electricity that computers use for energy.

_____

4

Car exhaust and smoke from factories cause (land pollution.)

_____

5

By melting down aluminum cans, we can (reduce) them to make new aluminum products.

_____

260

Answer Key: 1. can be replaced easily 2. Fossil fuels 3. nonrenewable resource 4. air pollution 5. recycle

© Houghton Mifflin Harcourt Publishing Company   (t) ©blickwinkel/Alamy Images; (bc) ©Getty Images; (tc) ©Grzegorz Petrykowski/Alamy Images

Word Play

Name _____

1 Use the words in the box to complete the puzzle.

Across

1. When you_____ something, it is broken down and made into something new.

8. You can_____ everyday items like grocery bags to prevent them from polluting the land.

9. Things that are useful to humans and come from nature are called _____.

Down

2. The practice of saving resources by using them wisely is called _____.

3. Introducing harmful materials into the environment causes _____.

4. Energy resources that were formed from the remains of organisms that lived long ago are called _____.

5. Natural resources that cannot be reused or renewed are called _____ resources.

6. Natural resources that can be replaced easily are called _____ resources.

7. In order to help conserve fossil fuels, _____ your use of them.

| natural resources* | renewable* | nonrenewable* | fossil fuels* | **reduce** |
| conservation* | **reuse** | pollution* | **recycle** | |

* Key Lesson Vocabulary

Apply Concepts

2 Circle the renewable resources. Mark an X on the nonrenewable resources.

solar power

vegetables

wood

wind power

natural gas

oil

3 Identify each situation as an example of reducing, reusing, or recycling.

1. Jake uses a plastic grocery bag to pick up trash. _____

2. Aluminum soda cans are melted down to make other aluminum cans. _____

3. Rei walks to school instead of riding in a car. _____

4. Terry uses old gift wrap to wrap a birthday present. _____

Take It Home!

Share with your family what you have learned about resources. With a family member, find examples of resources that you have seen or that you use at home.

Name _____

Essential Question

How Can We Conserve Resources?

Set a Purpose
What will you learn in this activity?

_____

_____

Think About the Procedure
Why are you asked to collect all the paper you would usually throw away?

_____

_____

Why do you think you should weigh the paper for this activity?

_____

_____

_____

_____

_____

Record Your Data
Record the weight of the paper collected each day for three weeks.

	Week 1	Week 2	Week 3
M			
T			
W			
Th			
F			
Total			

Make a bar graph to compare the total weight of paper for each week.

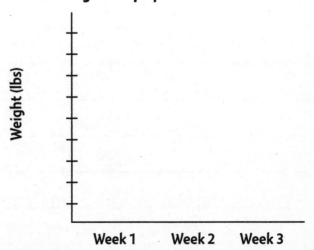

Weight (lbs)

Week 1   Week 2   Week 3

Draw Conclusions

How did the amount of paper you collected change each week? Why?

_____

_____

_____

_____

Analyze and Extend

1. What did you learn from collecting paper for three weeks?

_____

_____

_____

_____

_____

2. What are some ways to reuse different types of paper so it doesn't end up in the garbage?

_____

_____

_____

_____

_____

3. How many pounds of paper did you collect in all?

_____

_____

4. What are some ways you can think of to reduce the amount of wasted paper in your community and increase the amount of paper that is recycled?

_____

_____

_____

_____

_____

5. Think of another question you would like to answer about recycling paper.

_____

_____

_____

264

Essential Question

What Is Soil?

🧠 Engage Your Brain!

Find the answer to the following question in this lesson and record it here.

Why is soil important to these peach trees and to people?

_____

_____

_____

Active Reading

Lesson Vocabulary

List the terms. As you learn about each one, make notes in the Interactive Glossary.

_____ _____

_____ _____

_____ _____

Compare and Contrast

Many ideas in this lesson are connected because they explain comparisons and contrasts—how things are alike and different. Active readers stay focused on comparisons and contrasts when they ask themselves, How are things alike? How are they different?

Soil Is Not Just Dirt

Soil is important. Why? Most plants need soil to grow. Without plants, there would be no food for animals or people.

Active Reading As you read these two pages, draw a star next to what you think is the most important sentence. Be ready to explain why you think so.

When you are in a forest or garden, or even a parking lot, what is under your feet? Below the sticks, rocks, plants, and pavement, there is soil. **Soil** is a mixture of water, air, tiny pieces of rock, and humus. **Humus** is a rich mixture of the decomposed, or broken down, remains of plants and animals.

There are many kinds of soil. Soil can be black, red, brown, gray, and even white. Soil can be moist or dry. It can contain different kinds of minerals—even gold!

Soil is a mixture of decomposing plants and animals, small bits of rock, air, and water.

Some kinds of soil are better for growing plants than other kinds. Soil that is very good for plants is *fertile*. It can take hundreds or even thousands of years to form. Because soil is such an important natural resource, it must be conserved.

The dead leaves on this forest floor will decompose and become part of the soil.

Farmers must take care of the soil so it will remain fertile.

Soil Is a Natural Resource

Why is soil important to people and animals?

_____

_____

_____

_____

_____

How Does Soil Form?

If you dig deep into the soil, you can see that soil has different layers.

Active Reading As you read these two pages, draw one line under a cause. Draw two lines under the effect.

The top layer of soil is called *topsoil*. It is the most fertile soil layer. Plants grow in the topsoil. Topsoil is fertile because it contains humus. Humus makes the soil darker.

The layer beneath topsoil is called *subsoil*. Subsoil does not have a lot of humus, but it does have small pieces of rock. If you dig deep enough into the soil, you will reach solid rock. This is *bedrock*.

How does soil form? It forms from bedrock. When bedrock is at Earth's surface, it breaks down by weathering. Rain, wind, and other things weather bedrock, so big pieces of rock get smaller and smaller. Eventually, bedrock is broken into small bits of rock. These mix with air, water, and humus to form soil.

Soil Layers

Bedrock is solid rock. The small pieces of rock in the upper layers of soil come from bedrock.

Surface litter such as leaves, sticks, and rocks lies on top of soil. Plants and animals can be found above the soil and inside the soil, too.

Topsoil is the layer of soil closest to Earth's surface. Topsoil is where most plants grow. Topsoil is fertile because it contains humus. It also contains small bits of weathered bedrock.

Subsoil is one or more layers of soil that lie between the topsoil and bedrock. Subsoil contains slightly larger pieces of rock than topsoil and little or no humus.

Describe the Layers

Complete the chart by describing each layer of soil.

Topsoil	_____ _____ _____ _____
Subsoil	_____ _____ _____ _____
Bedrock	_____ _____ _____ _____

Types of Soil

There are more than 70,000 kinds of soil in the United States alone! What makes them different from one another?

Active Reading As you read these two pages, draw boxes around the names of things that are being contrasted.

As you know, soil contains humus as well as water, air, and bits of rock. One way to distinguish among soils is by the sizes of their particles.

Tiny particles of rock that you can see with just your eyes are called **sand**. **Silt** is tiny particles of rock that are difficult to see with only your eyes. Particles of rock that are even smaller than silt are called **clay**.

The amounts of sand, silt, and clay in soil give it texture. Texture is how the soil feels in your hands. Soil with more sand feels rough, while soil with more clay feels smooth. Soils can be made up of different minerals, depending on the area where the soils formed. A soil's color also depends on where it formed.

Most soils contain all three kinds of soil particles.

Soils that contain a lot of clay particles are fertile but heavy and sticky. They hold moisture well. They get very cold in winter, but dry out and get hard in the summer.

Sandy soils let water pass through easily. They dry out quickly. Sandy soils are usually light and easy to dig.

Soils that are mostly silt feel slippery when they are wet. They hold moisture for a long time. They also hold nutrients very well.

▶ Why does water pass through sandy soils more quickly than through soils that contain mostly clay or silt?

_____

_____

Plants Need Soil

What do plants get from soil? They get nutrients, water, and a place to live.

Active Reading As you read these two pages, find and underline the definition of *nutrients*.

Plants need water and light to grow. They also need nutrients. **Nutrients** are substances that plants take in from the soil through their roots to help them live and grow.

The best kind of soil for most plants is called *loam*. Loam has a balance of silt, sand, and clay. It is rich in nutrients and humus, it stays moist, and it is easy to dig. Some plants, though, grow better in other types of soil.

Plants take in nutrients and water from the soil through their roots.

Cabbage grows well in clay soils.

Sea grapes and sea oats grow on sandy beaches.

Which Soil Matches the Plant?

Look at the images above. What can you conclude about the soil requirements of these plants?

_____

_____

_____

In which of these soils do most types of cactus grow? What does this tell you about cactuses?

_____

_____

Composting

Don't throw away that banana peel! You can use fruit peels and other kitchen scraps to help plants grow.

Active Reading As you read these two pages, find and underline two facts about compost.

Compost is humus that you make yourself. Pile plant parts, such as dried leaves and grass, into a big container. Then add scraps of fruits and vegetables. Tiny organisms too small to see will decompose the scraps to make humus. Spread compost on your plants so they will grow quickly and stay healthy.

Compost does more than help plants in your garden. Making compost means that you don't throw away as much garbage. When people throw away less garbage, that's good for everyone!

Add things like eggshells, peelings, and fruits and vegetables to compost. You can even add newspaper. Don't add animal products such as meat and cheese.

Do the Math!
Use Subtraction

It can take 850 years for 2 cm of soil to form. It can take 6 months to make 2 cm of compost for your garden. How much longer does it take soil to form than it does to make compost?

_____

_____

Sum It Up!

When you're done, use the answer key to check and revise your work.

The blue words in each summary statement are incorrect. Write words to replace the blue parts.

1 Compost is material that helps plants grow because it is contains a lot of clay.

_____

2  Soil is made quickly in nature.

_____

3 Plants need soil for support and light.

_____

4  Weathering causes humus below the soil to break into smaller pieces.

_____

5  Silty soil contains the largest particles of rock.

_____

6 Topsoil is so important to plant growth around the world that people do not need to conserve it.

_____

Brain Check

Name _____

Word Play

1 Use the words in the box to complete the puzzle.

soil*	humus*	sand*	silt*	clay*	nutrients*
bedrock	loam	compost	plants		*Key Lesson Vocabulary

Across

1. The type of soil that drains water most quickly _____

3. Living things that need soil for support _____

5. The type of soil that holds water for the longest time _____

6. The type of soil that has tiny particles of rock bigger than clay but smaller than sand _____

7. This is weathered by wind and water to make soil. _____

8. Something found in soil that is made of dead plants and animals
_____

Down

1. This provides plants with the water and nutrients they need to survive. _____

2. This is the best kind of soil for plants. It is made of the three soil types. _____

4. Substances in soil that plants need to grow _____

5. Can be made using kitchen scraps and dead plants _____

© Houghton Mifflin Harcourt Publishing Company ©Digital Vision/Getty Images

277

Apply Concepts

2 Answer the questions about the picture.

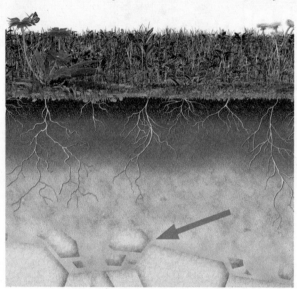

Explain why you can see darker soil toward the top of the soil layers.

_____

_____

_____

_____

What is happening where the red arrow is pointing?

_____

_____

3 Fill in the blanks to make the statements true.

When bedrock breaks down for a long time and mixes with air, water, and the decomposed remains of _____ , soil is formed. Soil is a resource because plants need it to _____ , and we depend on plants for our _____ . Soil supports plants and gives them the _____ they need to grow.

Take It Home!

With an adult, look at the soil in your yard or at a park. Which type of soil is it? Is it a mixture? Write down your observations and share them with the class.

Meet the Environmental Scientists

Noah Idechong

Noah Idechong grew up in a small fishing village on the island nation of Palau. Palauan children are taught to take special care of the ocean. The ocean provides their families with food. Idechong works to conserve ocean life. Boats can damage coral on the coast. When the coral dies, many fish leave, and the fish populations get smaller. Idechong helps make rules to protect the coastal environment.

Many kinds of fish swim in island waters. By putting limits on fishing in certain areas, more fish can survive and reproduce.

Lena Qiying Ma

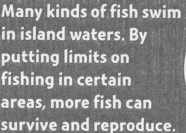

Lena Qiying Ma is a soil scientist. She studies how some plants take in arsenic [AR•suh•nik]. Arsenic is used as a poison to keep weeds away from crops. During her research, Ma found a fern growing in an industrial site. It was green even though the soil was polluted with arsenic. Ma discovered that ferns remove arsenic from soil. She studies how the fern can be used to clean up pollution in soil and groundwater.

This scientist is measuring a soil property called pH. Different types of plants grow best at different pH ranges. This property is important for brake ferns, because it can affect the amount of arsenic these plants can take in.

Be a Soil Scientist!

A farmer is planting his crops. He tests the pH of the soil from different fields on his farm. He wants to know which crop to plant in each field.

Sugar beets grow best in soil that has a pH around 8.

Blueberries grow best in soil that has a pH around 4.

Broccoli grows best in soil that has a pH around 6.

Use the pH scale below to match the soil from each field with the best crop to plant in that field. Write the name of the crop on the line for the correct soil.

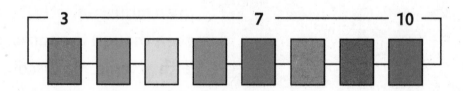

3 — 7 — 10

Technology at Work:

Problems and Fixes

In the past, many soft drinks came in glass bottles. Today, most soft drinks come in aluminum cans. Aluminum cans are lighter than glass and do not break. But aluminum is a nonrenewable resource. Recycling technology helps solve this problem.

From a recycling bin, used cans go to recycling centers.

Machines crush the cans. The flat cans form blocks of aluminum.

The blocks are melted and rolled into thin sheets. Then the aluminum is made into new cans and other items. Aluminum can be recycled over and over.

How does recycling help solve problems caused by using aluminum cans?

_____

_____

_____

Solve a Problem

Technology can solve problems. It can also cause problems. Today, millions of products are made from plastic, including water bottles, pens, toys, and bags. But plastic is made from fossil fuels, which are nonrenewable resources. Also, plastic does not break down easily.

Cars help people get around. But they cause air pollution.

Think of a product you use that is made from plastic. Draw your product below.

What problem does your product cause? How can technology help solve this problem?

_____

_____

_____

Build On It!

Rise to the engineering design challenge—complete **Redesign It: Reduce Packaging** on the Inquiry Flipchart.

Unit 6 Review

Vocabulary Review

Use the terms in the box to complete the sentences.

> conservation
> humus
> nutrients
> pollution
> soil

1. A part of soil with a rich mixture of decomposing plants and animals is _____.

2. Turning off lights and recycling are examples of _____.

3. A mixture of minerals, air, water, and humus is _____.

4. Garbage on the land and chemicals in the air are types of _____.

5. To grow, plants need water, light, and _____ from the soil.

Science Concepts

Fill in the letter of the choice that best answers the question.

6. Which source of energy is a renewable resource?

   Ⓐ coal
   Ⓑ natural gas
   Ⓒ oil
   Ⓓ wind

7. How can you reduce your use of natural resources?

   Ⓐ place your empty cereal box in the recycling bin
   Ⓑ place your lunch in a reusable box instead of a paper bag
   Ⓒ plant a tree to replace the tree used for firewood
   Ⓓ take old leaves to the dump

Science Concepts

Fill in the letter of the choice that best answers the question.

8. Hector wants to put some soil in a pot that will drain water quickly. Which soil particle should be the largest part of the soil?

- Ⓐ clay
- Ⓑ humus
- Ⓒ sand
- Ⓓ silt

9. The graph below shows the percentage of aluminum cans that are recycled.

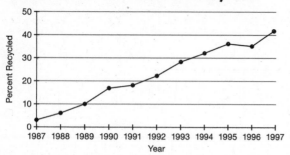

Which **best** explains the data in the line graph?

- Ⓐ The number of recycling bins is increasing.
- Ⓑ The number of cans being used is increasing.
- Ⓒ The percentage of cans recycled is increasing.
- Ⓓ The number of people recycling cans is increasing.

10. Tyrone wants to make sure his soil is mostly clay particles. What should he look for?

- Ⓐ The soil will dry out quickly.
- Ⓑ The soil will be heavy and sticky.
- Ⓒ The soil will feel slippery when wet.
- Ⓓ The soil will have small particles that he can see.

11. Which is an example of reusing?

- Ⓐ carpooling to soccer practice
- Ⓑ turning off lights when not in use
- Ⓒ taking cloth bags to the grocery store to carry groceries back home
- Ⓓ putting a plastic bottle in the recycling bin

12. Abbey and her family collected newspapers in the bin below.

Which word **best** describes what they are doing?

- Ⓐ nutrients
- Ⓑ pollution
- Ⓒ recycling
- Ⓓ renewing

13. Which is an effect of burning fossil fuels?

Ⓐ conservation

Ⓑ pollution

Ⓒ recycling

Ⓓ reusing

14. Giorgio made the soil model below.

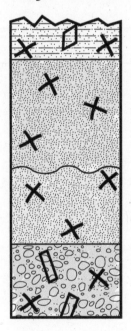

Which names the top layer in his drawing?

Ⓐ bedrock

Ⓑ silt

Ⓒ subsoil

Ⓓ topsoil

15. Why is loam the best kind of soil for plants?

Ⓐ It is rich in nutrients to help the plants grow.

Ⓑ It is heavy and thick, so it supports the plants.

Ⓒ It has the most sand, so water drains quickly.

Ⓓ It has more air pockets, so it allows in light to the roots.

16. Which resource is a fossil fuel?

Ⓐ coal

Ⓑ paper

Ⓒ firewood

Ⓓ sun

17. Look at the picture below.

What are these examples of?

Ⓐ conservation

Ⓑ humus

Ⓒ nonrenewable resources

Ⓓ pollution

Apply Inquiry and Review the Big Idea

Write the answers to these questions.

18. Look at the drawing below.

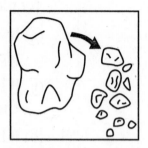

What process is shown in this drawing? How can soil form from this process?

_____

_____

_____

19. Ms. Gomez's class is doing some community service.

What natural resource are they conserving? How else can they conserve this natural resource?

_____

_____

_____

Water and Weather

Big Idea

Water is important to all living things in many different ways. The sun is the source of energy for the water cycle and weather.

frozen waterfall with icicles

I Wonder Why

Why does a frozen waterfall start to flow once the sun comes out? *Turn the page to find out.*

Here's why The frozen waterfall will flow when the sun comes out. This is because the sun's energy adds heat to the ice. The ice changes its state from a solid to a liquid. Liquid water will flow.

In this unit, you will explore the Big Idea, the Essential Questions, and the Investigations on the Inquiry Flipchart.

Levels of Inquiry Key ■ DIRECTED ■ GUIDED ■ INDEPENDENT

Track Your Progress

Big Idea Water is important to all living things in many different ways. The sun is the source of energy for the water cycle and weather.

Essential Questions

Now I Get the Big Idea!

Science Notebook

Before you begin each lesson, be sure to write your thoughts about the Essential Question.

Essential Question
What Is the Water Cycle?

Engage Your Brain!

Find the answer to the following question in this lesson and record it here.

You can see mist above the lake's surface. Where did it come from?

_____

_____

_____

Active Reading

Lesson Vocabulary
List the terms. As you learn about each one, make notes in the Interactive Glossary.

_____ _____

_____ _____

_____ _____

Compare and Contrast
Many ideas in this lesson are connected because they explain how things compare and contrast. Active readers stay focused on comparisons and contrasts when they ask themselves, How are these things alike? How are they different?

Water Moves All Around

If you were in a spaceship looking down at Earth, you would see that most of Earth is covered by water.

Active Reading As you read this page, find and underline two examples of fresh water.

Almost all water on Earth is in the oceans. Ocean water is **salt water**, which contains salt, of course! It is too salty for us to drink. However, many life forms live in salt water.

Only a tiny part of Earth's water is fresh water. **Fresh water** has very little salt in it. We need fresh water to drink. Many plants and animals need fresh water, too. Rivers and lakes contain fresh water, but most of Earth's fresh water is frozen!

Ocean water

Water is needed for life. About three-fourths of Earth is covered by water. Most of that water is in the oceans.

Icebergs in an ocean

Icebergs are made of fresh water. Most of Earth's fresh water is frozen in glaciers at the South Pole. That's why it's important to conserve the fresh water that is not frozen.

Waterfall

Fresh water flows in this waterfall. Much of Earth's fresh water is above ground, but some fresh water is underground.

Lake

This lake contains fresh water. Lakes provide drinking water to many animals. Most plants need fresh water. Many kinds of fish, frogs, snails, and other animals live in and around fresh water.

Do the Math!
Find the Fraction

Only 3 out of every 100 liters of water on Earth is fresh water. What fraction of Earth's water is fresh water?

_____

Three Forms of Water

Water is a kind of matter. It can exist as a solid, a liquid, or a gas.

Active Reading When things are contrasted, you find out ways they are different. Draw boxes around three things that are being contrasted.

Ice is solid water. Icebergs are small chunks of ice in the ocean. Glaciers are huge blocks of ice. Some glaciers are as big as whole countries! Most of Earth's fresh water is ice.

Ice melts to make liquid water. Liquid water is found in the ocean, rivers, streams, ponds, and even underground.

When water exists as a gas, it is called *water vapor*. Water vapor is in the air we breathe. You cannot see water vapor.

> Water can exist as a solid, a liquid, or a gas.

© Houghton Mifflin Harcourt Publishing Company (b) ©Comstock/Getty Images

States of Water

Water vapor

Air is a mixture of gases. One of these gases is water vapor. You can't see water vapor. The space between the clouds has water vapor in it.

Liquid water

Liquid water fills the ocean, lakes, and streams. Clouds are made of small droplets of liquid water. Fog, mist, and falling rain are also liquid water.

Ice

This glacier is an example of ice, Earth's solid water. Glaciers cover land that is close to the North Pole and the South Pole. They also cover some mountains.

Where Is the Water?

1. Where can you find water vapor in nature?

   _____

2. Where can you find liquid water in nature?

   _____

   _____

3. Where can you find solid water in nature?

   _____

Changing States

Water changes state. For example, liquid water can change to ice and to water vapor. What causes water to change state?

Active Reading Find sentences that contrast two things. Draw a line under each sentence.

Water changes state when it is heated or cooled. When enough heat is added to ice, it becomes liquid water. This change of state is called *melting*. The reverse of melting is *freezing*.

When liquid water gains enough heat, it evaporates to become water vapor. **Evaporation** is the change of state from a liquid to a gas.

When water vapor loses enough heat, it changes back to liquid water. The change of state from a gas to a liquid is called **condensation**. Condensation and evaporation are opposite processes.

For water vapor to condense, it needs something to condense on. Even the drops of water in clouds have condensed on tiny pieces of dust.

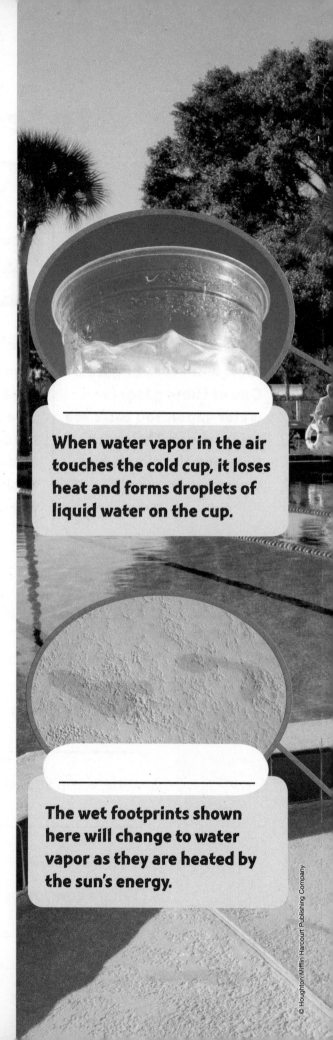

When water vapor in the air touches the cold cup, it loses heat and forms droplets of liquid water on the cup.

The wet footprints shown here will change to water vapor as they are heated by the sun's energy.

Finding Evaporation and Condensation

Look at the photos on these pages. Label the photos as either condensation or evaporation.

_____

After a cool night, you may wake up to find water droplets called dew covering the grass. This happens when water vapor in the air that is directly above the cool ground forms water droplets on the grass.

The Water Cycle

Water is always moving. In fact, water moves continuously from Earth's surface to the atmosphere and back to Earth.

Active Reading A cause tells why something happens. Draw one line under each cause.

The sun heats the ocean. This causes water to evaporate and become water vapor. The water vapor mixes with other gases and moves high up in the air.

As the water vapor rises, it cools. If it loses enough heat energy, it condenses to form water droplets in clouds. This water can fall back to Earth as **precipitation**. Precipitation can be rain, sleet, snow, or hail. The type of precipitation that falls depends on the temperature of the air around it.

After water falls, it moves across land. Some water flows underground. This is *groundwater*. Groundwater and surface water flow back to the ocean. More water in the ocean is heated and evaporates again. This never-ending movement of water between Earth's surface and the air is called the **water cycle**.

The sun's energy warms the surface of the ocean or other bodies of water. Some of the water evaporates and enters the air as water vapor.

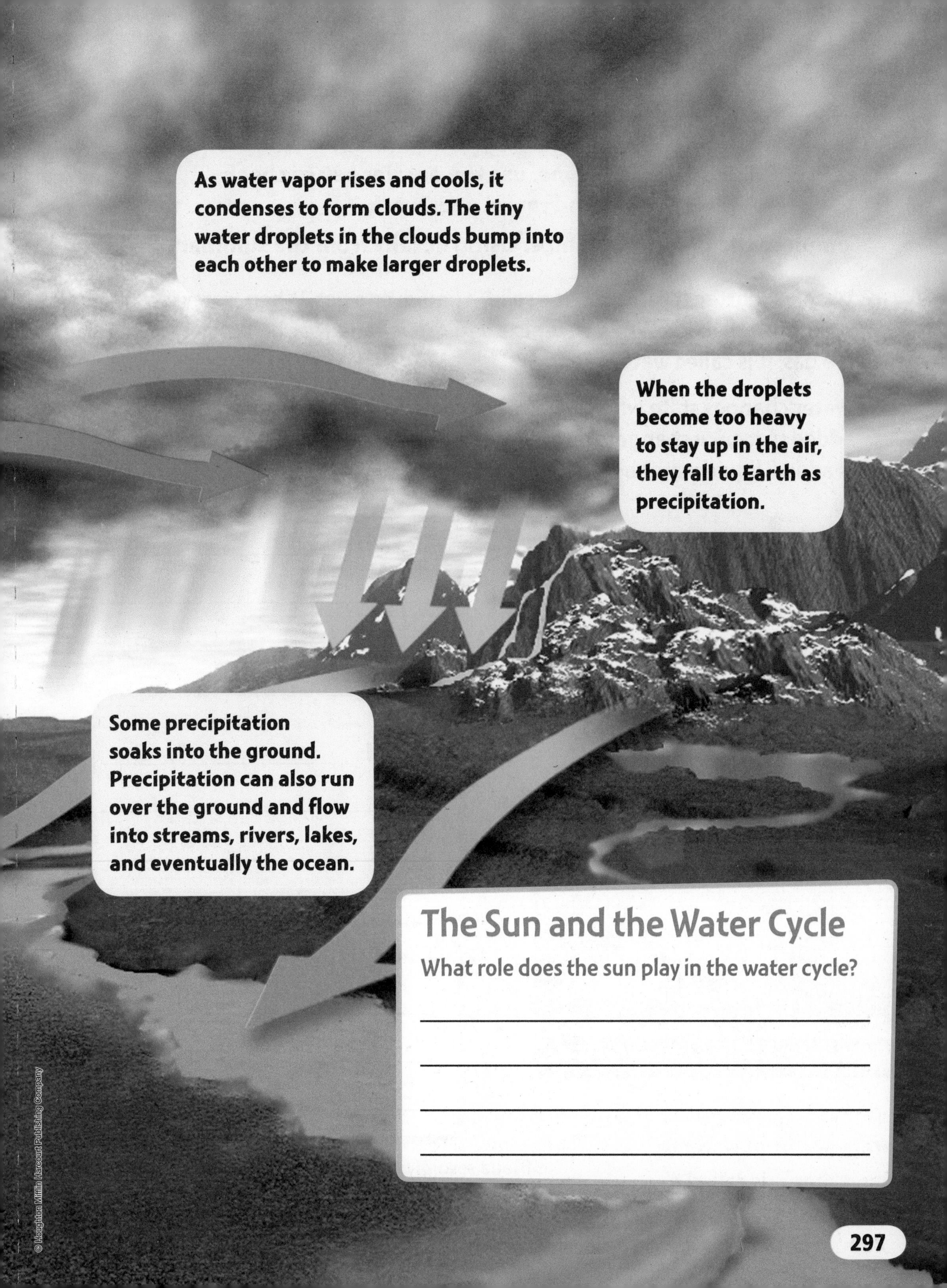

As water vapor rises and cools, it condenses to form clouds. The tiny water droplets in the clouds bump into each other to make larger droplets.

When the droplets become too heavy to stay up in the air, they fall to Earth as precipitation.

Some precipitation soaks into the ground. Precipitation can also run over the ground and flow into streams, rivers, lakes, and eventually the ocean.

The Sun and the Water Cycle
What role does the sun play in the water cycle?

_____

_____

_____

_____

Sum It Up!

When you're done, use the answer key to check
and revise your work.

Complete the graphic organizer using details from the summary below.

Water is matter. It can exist as a solid, a liquid, or a gas. When water is a solid, it is called ice. When water is a liquid, it is called water. When water is a gas, it is called water vapor.

Water changes state when it warms or cools. For example, when heat is added to ice, ice changes state to become liquid water. If even more heat is added, liquid water becomes water vapor.

Main Idea
Water can exist in three states: solid, liquid, and gas.

1 Detail: _____
_____
_____

2 Detail: _____
_____
_____

3 Detail: _____
_____
_____
_____

Name _____

Word Play

1 Unscramble each word and write it in the boxes.

1. **TASL TAWRE**
   Clue: Earth is mostly covered with this

   ☐☐☐☐☐ ☐☐Ⓞ☐Ⓞ

2. **NOCENDASNOIT**
   Clue: When water vapor becomes liquid

   ☐☐Ⓞ☐☐☐Ⓞ☐☐Ⓞ☐☐

3. **ARTEW AVOPR**
   Clue: What evaporating water becomes

   ☐☐☐Ⓞ☐ Ⓞ☐☐Ⓞ☐

4. **TEARW EYCCL**
   Clue: The movement of water from ocean to land and back

   ☐Ⓞ☐☐☐ ☐☐☐ⓄⓄ

5. **CIPERPNOITITA**
   Clue: Water that falls from the sky

   Ⓞ☐Ⓞ☐☐☐☐☐☐Ⓞ☐☐

6. **EHSFR REAWT**
   Clue: Found in rivers and lakes

   ☐Ⓞ☐☐☐ ☐Ⓞ☐☐☐

7. **TERWADNGROU**
   Clue: What flows underground

   Ⓞ☐Ⓞ☐☐☐☐☐☐☐☐

Write the letters in the circles on the lines below.
Unscramble them to form two more words.

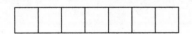

_____

_____

8. Clue: One form of frozen water at the South Pole

   ☐☐☐☐☐☐

9. Clue: When liquid water becomes water vapor

   ☐☐☐☐☐☐☐☐☐☐

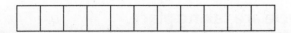

Apply Concepts

2 Look at the picture of the water cycle. Add labels to show three processes that are part of the water cycle. Label the salt water and the fresh water.

2. _____

1. _____

3. _____

5. _____

4. _____

3 What gives water the energy it needs to move around the world in the water cycle?

_____

Take It Home!

Share what you have learned about the water cycle with your family. With a family member, look around for places where processes from the water cycle are taking place.

6 Things You Should Know About Hydrologists

1 Hydrologists study the quality and movement of water on Earth.

2 They care about and protect the water in rivers, streams, and oceans.

3 Hydrologists test water to make sure it is safe to drink or swim in.

4 They help cities and farms get the amount of water they need.

5 They also help prevent problems from floods and droughts.

6 Hydrologists help design dams to make electricity and sewers to drain water.

Be a Hydrologist!

Answer these five questions about hydrologists.

1

What do hydrologists study?

_____

_____

_____

_____

2

Why do hydrologists test our drinking water?

_____

_____

_____

3

How do hydrologists help farmers?

_____

_____

_____

4

How do hydrologists help cities?

_____

_____

_____

_____

5

Write and answer your own question about hydrologists.

_____

_____

_____

_____

_____

©Houghton Mifflin Harcourt Publishing Company   (bg) ©Comstock/Getty Images

Essential Question

What Is Weather?

🧠 Engage Your Brain!

Find the answer to the following question in this lesson and record it here.

How could the weather in this city be measured?

_____

_____

_____

_____

_____

Active Reading

Lesson Vocabulary

List the terms. As you learn about each one, make notes in the Interactive Glossary.

_____ _____

_____ _____

Using Headings

Active readers preview headings and use them to pose questions that establish purposes for reading. Reading with a purpose helps active readers focus on understanding and recalling what they read in order to fulfill the purpose.

A World of Weather

The sun's energy causes the water cycle. It also affects the weather. As the sun heats Earth, temperatures change. Changing temperatures mean changing weather!

Active Reading As you read these two pages, underline lesson vocabulary each time it is used.

Earth is surrounded by a layer of gases. This layer of gases is Earth's **atmosphere**. **Oxygen** is one of the gases in Earth's atmosphere. Most living things need oxygen to survive. Water vapor is another type of gas in Earth's atmosphere.

Conditions in the atmosphere can change. **Weather** is the condition of the atmosphere at any one place and time. If the atmosphere over your school is warm and dry in the morning, your weather is warm and dry. But the atmosphere, and your weather, could change. The weather could be cool and rainy by the afternoon.

This cloud is a *cumulonimbus* [kyoo•myuh•loh•NIM•buhs] cloud. These clouds are often tall and have a flat top. They sometimes look like mushrooms and often produce thunderstorms.

Types of Clouds

There are many types of clouds. Each type of cloud has a different shape. The type of clouds in the sky can tell you what kind of weather may be coming.

Cirrus [SIR•uhs] clouds are thin and feathery. Cirrus clouds form high up in the atmosphere, where temperatures are cold. They are often a sign that the weather is about to change.

Cumulus [KYOO•myuh•luhs] clouds have flat bottoms and are puffy on top. They look like piles of cotton. Cumulus clouds usually mean fair weather, but they can develop into cumulonimbus clouds.

Stratus clouds look like thin blankets. Often, they hang low in the atmosphere. Stratus clouds can mean that light rain or snow is coming.

▶ Suppose the weather is fair. What type of clouds might you see in the atmosphere? Draw and label them.

Measuring Weather

It's okay to say, "It's cold and rainy outside." But when we need to know exactly what the weather is, we must measure it.

Active Reading As you read this page, turn the heading into a question in your mind and circle sentences that answer the question.

Temperature is a measure of how hot or cold something is. The tool we use to measure temperature is a *thermometer*. Air temperature is measured in degrees Celsius (°C) or degrees Fahrenheit (°F).

The temperature of the atmosphere affects the kind of precipitation that falls. Above 0 °C, rain is likely. Below 0 °C, the air is so cold that rain, sleet, or snow may fall.

Sometimes it rains so much that it's hard to see anything. A *rain gauge* is a tool that collects rain and shows how much has fallen.

If the wind is blowing, we can tell the direction it's coming from with a *wind vane*. A *wind meter* tells how fast the wind is blowing.

Thermometer

A thermometer is a tube filled with a liquid. When the air gets hotter, the liquid moves up the tube. When the air gets cooler, the liquid moves down the tube. To find the temperature, read the number next to the top of the liquid.

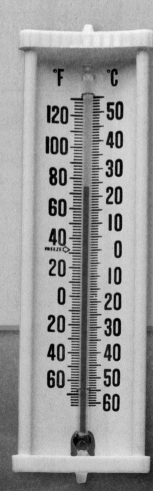

Rain gauge

A rain gauge measures rainfall. How do you read a rain gauge? Look at the water in the gauge. Read the number where the water lines up with the scale. Rain can be measured in centimeters or inches. A rain gauge is emptied after each use to measure more rainfall.

Wind vane

A wind vane shows the way the wind is blowing. The bird below looks in the direction the wind is coming from. The wind can come from the east, west, north, south, or somewhere in between.

▶ Read the instruments and record the temperature, rain amount, and wind direction on the lines provided.

Wind meter

A wind meter measures how fast the wind blows.

Do the Math!

Solve a Word Problem

At 9:00 a.m., the air temperature was 18 °C. By 4:00 p.m., it had risen to 32 °C. How much warmer was it at 4:00 p.m. than at 9:00 a.m.?

Being Ready For Weather

Weather affects us in many ways. We have to consider weather when we choose what to wear, what items to use, and where to go.

To stay safe and comfortable, we wear clothing that's right for the weather. When it's raining, we stay dry with a raincoat, boots, and umbrella.

The weather also affects the activities we can do. We can swim when it's warm. We can ski only when it's cold enough for snow.

To help us, scientists try to predict the weather. When we know what kind of weather is coming, we can make plans to dress right, and we can choose the right kinds of activities.

This child is wearing the right clothes and using an umbrella to stay safe and comfortable in the rain.

This child is using the right items to stay safe and comfortable during a hot, sunny day at the beach.

What to Wear

Look at each item. In what type of weather do you need each of these? How does each item protect you from the weather?

winter hat

_____

_____

_____

sunglasses

_____

_____

Watch Out For Weather!

Weather can be severe and even dangerous. Hurricanes, thunderstorms, tornadoes, and blizzards are examples of severe weather.

Active Reading As you read this page, find and underline examples of severe weather.

A *hurricane* is a tropical storm with winds of 119 kilometers (74 miles) per hour or more. Hurricanes form over warm ocean water. They become slow, large storms soon after they reach land. Hurricanes can blow trees over and cause large areas of flooding.

Thunderstorms are strong storms that have thunder and lightning. Often there is heavy rain and strong wind, too.

Tornadoes are small, spinning columns of very strong wind.

A *blizzard* is a snowstorm with strong wind and a very low temperature.

To be safe in severe weather, follow directions from a teacher, parent, or other adult who knows what to do.

Tornado

Tornadoes are most common in states, such as Texas and Kansas, where there are large plains. Tornado winds are so strong that they can rip a tree out of the ground and move a car through the air.

Blizzard

During blizzards, the snow blows so fast it is hard to see through. Being out in a blizzard is cold and dangerous!

Thunderstorm

Lightning is a flash of electricity that happens during a thunderstorm. Lightning can kill people. Always stay indoors during a thunderstorm.

Hurricane

Since hurricanes form over warm ocean waters, they lose power quickly when they move over land. But hurricanes can still do a lot of damage when they reach land.

Staying Safe In Severe Weather

Sara thinks that thunderstorms are exciting. She wants to go outside during one. Sara asks her mother to go with her. What should Sara's mother tell her?

_____

_____

_____

Sum It Up!

When you're done, use the answer key to check and revise your work.

Write the vocabulary term that matches each photo and caption.

1

This tool is used to measure how much rain has fallen.

_____

2

This tool is used to measure the direction of wind.

_____

3

This tool is used to measure the temperature of the air.

_____

Summarize

Fill in the missing words to tell about weather.

You can recognize clouds by their (4) _____. (5) _____

clouds are thin and wispy. Clouds that look like thin blankets are

(6) _____ clouds. The clouds that look like piles of cotton are

(7) _____ clouds. Each different type of cloud means a different type

of weather is coming. Stratus clouds usually mean that light (8) _____

or snow is coming. If you see a cumulus cloud, you know that (9) _____

weather is coming. Some weather can be severe. (10) _____ form over

ocean water. Strong winds and lots of snow occur during a (11) _____.

Answer Key: 1. rain gauge **2.** wind vane **3.** thermometer **4.** shapes **5.** Cirrus **6.** stratus **7.** cumulus **8.** rain **9.** fair **10.** Hurricanes **11.** blizzard

Word Play

1

Read the clues. Unscramble the words to complete the sentence.

1. You use a thermometer to measure air __ __ __ __ __ __ __ __ __ __ __.	etmrepatuer
2. The gases that surround Earth make up the __ __ __ __ __ __ __ __ __ __.	hperesmoat
3. One type of gas in the atmosphere is __ __ __ __ __ __.	negoyx
4. The condition of the atmosphere at one place and time is the __ __ __ __ __ __ __.	rwehate
5. Fast wind that moves in a spiral is a __ __ __ __ __ __ __.	troanod
6. You measure wind direction with a __ __ __ __ __ __ __ __ __.	diwn vean

Apply Concepts

2 Draw yourself measuring the weather. Show the tool or tools that you use. Describe how to use each measuring tool that you draw.

_____

_____

_____

_____

_____

_____

3 Label the pictures of severe weather. Draw a line from each label to the correct description of the severe weather.

_____   _____   _____

| Starts over the ocean; strong wind and rain | Thunder, lightning, and usually rain | Lots of snow and wind; very cold |

Take It Home!

Watch the weather forecast for the next week with an adult. Measure the week's weather. Discuss whether or not the forecast was correct.

Name _____

Essential Question

How Can We Measure Weather?

Set a Purpose
What will you learn during this investigation?

_____
_____
_____
_____

Think About the Procedure
Which tools measure air temperature, wind direction, and rainfall? What is a weather condition that is not measured by these instruments?

_____
_____
_____
_____
_____

What are some things that might cause you to get an incorrect measurement?

_____
_____
_____
_____
_____

Record Your Data
Use the table to record weather data for the first week. Make similar tables in your Science Notebook to record data for weeks two and three.

	Temperature	Wind Direction	Amount of Rain
Monday			
Tuesday			
Wednesday			
Thursday			
Friday			

Draw Conclusions

How did the weather change over the three-week period? Use your data tables as a reference.

_____

_____

_____

_____

_____

_____

Analyze and Extend

1. Compare your data to the data of another group of students. Are your data the same? If not, how do you account for the differences?

_____

_____

_____

2. Make a weather prediction for the next two days.

_____

_____

_____

3. How did you use all of your collected data to make your weather prediction?

_____

_____

_____

_____

_____

4. How might you use a measurement of temperature, wind direction, or amount of rainfall?

_____

_____

_____

5. Think of other questions you would like to ask about measuring weather and making weather predictions.

_____

_____

_____

_____

_____

Keeping Dry:
Raincoat vs. Poncho

Often, more than one design can meet the same need. Each design may have different features. Compare the features of the raincoat and poncho below.

A raincoat with snaps or buttons fits more closely around the body. It does not blow around in the wind.

The poncho is cut large. It fits easily over any clothes.

The material is lightweight. It folds into a small package. It is easy to carry around.

Buttons tighten the ends of sleeves. This keeps water from getting in.

Pockets help keep objects dry in the rain.

When is the raincoat a better choice? When is the poncho a better choice? Explain.

_____

_____

_____

317

Design a Better Product

Think about the best parts of the raincoat and the poncho. Then create a new design using parts of both. Draw your design below.

Rain boots are other tools that help us stay dry.

Why is your product better than the raincoat or the poncho?

_____

_____

_____

Build On It!

Rise to the engineering design challenge—complete **Design It: Build a Wind Streamer** on the Inquiry Flipchart.

Unit 7 Review

Vocabulary Review

Use the terms in the box to complete the sentences.

> atmosphere
> condensation
> temperature
> water cycle
> weather

1. Sunny, cloudy, and windy are examples of different types of _____.

2. A drop of water moves around Earth from the land, to the air, to the sea, and even underground as part of the _____.

3. When weather forecasters talk about the air around Earth, they are referring to the _____.

4. On a very hot summer day, you can read the thermometer to find out the _____.

5. Water vapor changes into rain in the process of _____.

Science Concepts

Fill in the letter of the choice that best answers the question.

6. George cannot decide if he needs his umbrella today. He looks out the window and observes the clouds. Which kind of cloud would make George infer that a thunderstorm is in the forecast?

   Ⓐ cirrus

   Ⓑ stratus

   Ⓒ cumulus

   Ⓓ cumulonimbus

7. Rain falls on a cool morning. By late morning, the temperature increases, and the sun warms a puddle of water. Through evaporation, what does the puddle of water change to?

   Ⓐ gas

   Ⓑ ice

   Ⓒ rain

   Ⓓ snow

Science Concepts

Fill in the letter of the choice that best answers the question.

8. Water is important to the survival of plants, animals, and people. Why is salt water important to people?

   Ⓐ It provides air for people.

   Ⓑ It provides homes for people.

   Ⓒ It provides drinking water for people.

   Ⓓ It provides a habitat for some animals that people eat.

9. Ms. Greyson is a weather forecaster. On the news, she tells people there is a thunderstorm in the forecast. How can people prepare for this severe weather?

   Ⓐ stay inside a building in a safe room away from windows

   Ⓑ make sure indoor heating works

   Ⓒ make sure their snow blowers work

   Ⓓ use sheets to cover plants that might freeze

10. Antwan wants to record weather data at his house. He wants to measure the amount of precipitation and the wind speed. Which instruments should he use?

    Ⓐ a thermometer and a rain gauge

    Ⓑ a rain gauge and a wind meter

    Ⓒ a wind meter and a wind vane

    Ⓓ a thermometer and a wind vane

11. In the morning, it rained, leaving puddles in Camilla's driveway. An hour later, she noticed that the puddles that were in a sunny part of the driveway had dried up. The puddles in a shady part of the driveway were still there. The thermometers below show the temperatures in the two areas.

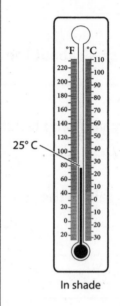
25° C

In shade

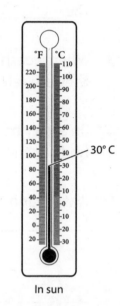
30° C

In sun

Which conclusion can Camilla draw from her observations?

   Ⓐ Puddles make temperatures fall.

   Ⓑ Evaporation makes temperatures rise.

   Ⓒ Heat makes water condense more quickly.

   Ⓓ Heat makes water evaporate more quickly.

12. Even though water makes up 75 percent of Earth, why is it so important to conserve water?

(A) The water we can drink makes up a small fraction of the water on Earth.

(B) The water where we gather food makes up a small fraction of the water on Earth.

(C) The water we swim in makes up a small fraction of the water on Earth.

(D) The water that is part of the water cycle makes up a small fraction of the water on Earth.

13. Mr. Rose's class just finished learning about the water cycle. The students understand the roles of evaporation and precipitation in the picture below. They need to review condensation.

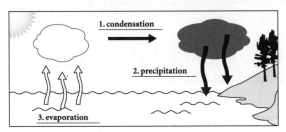

How would you describe the role of condensation in the picture above?

(A) The sun is heating the cool water.

(B) The rain is going into the groundwater.

(C) The air cools water vapor in the atmosphere.

(D) The rain moves from the land to air and underground.

14. The following calendar shows the weather in the month of May.

Which week in May had the most days of precipitation?

(A) the first week

(B) the second week

(C) the third week

(D) the fourth week

15. It is an afternoon in November. The thermometer reads 2 degrees Celsius. The wind meter measures the wind speed at 5 kilometers per hour. The clouds are thin and wispy. What is the weather outside?

(A) cold with high winds and sunny

(B) cold with little wind and sunny

(C) cold with little wind and snowy

(D) cold with high winds and rainy

Apply Inquiry and Review the Big Idea

Write the answers to these questions.

16. You can measure the temperature of the air with a thermometer. Describe three other types of weather measurements you could make and how you could measure them.

_____

_____

17. Below is the beginning of a five-day forecast.

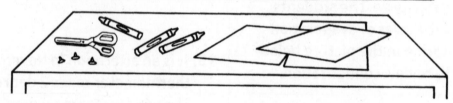

Our Weather				
Monday	Tuesday	Wednesday	Thursday	Friday
we think	we think			

You know that cold weather is coming after Tuesday. Complete the forecast for Wednesday. Explain why you predicted the weather that you did.

_____

_____

(fused) ©Pontus Johansson/Alamy Images; (border) ©NDisc/Age Fotostock (used) ©PSL Images/Alamy Images; (bg) ©NDisc/Age Fotostock

Houghton Mifflin Harcourt Publishing Company

UNIT 8

Earth and Its Moon

The motion of Earth and the moon causes repeating patterns that can be seen in nature, including day and night, seasons, and other cycles.

day and night on Earth

I Wonder Why

Why is it night on one side of Earth while it's day on the other? *Turn the page to find out.*

Here's why The Earth is always spinning around. As it turns, one part of Earth is in the sun's light while the other part of Earth is in a dark shadow.

In this unit, you will explore the Big Idea, the Essential Questions, and the Investigations on the Inquiry Flipchart.

Levels of Inquiry Key ■ DIRECTED ■ GUIDED ■ INDEPENDENT

Big Idea The motion of Earth and the moon causes repeating patterns that can be seen in nature, including day and night, seasons, and other cycles.

Track Your Progress

Essential Questions

Now I Get the Big Idea!

Science Notebook

Before you begin each lesson, be sure your thoughts about the Essential Que

Essential Question

How Do Earth and the Moon Move?

Engage Your Brain!

Find the answer to the following question in this lesson and record it here.

The ocean is reflecting light from the full moon. How is the moon acting on the ocean?

_____

Active Reading

Lesson Vocabulary

List the terms. As you learn about each one, make notes in the Interactive Glossary.

_____ _____

_____ _____

Sequence

Many ideas in this lesson are connected by a sequence, or order, that describes the steps in a process. Active readers stay focused on sequence when they mark the transition from one stage of an idea or step in a process to another.

Turning Through the Day

Look at your desk. Is it moving? It may not look like it, but everything in your classroom is moving—including you!

As you read these two pages, circle lesson vocabulary each time it is used.

Looking at Earth from above the North Pole, we see that Earth turns in the opposite direction to a clock. As Earth turns, half of it gets light from the sun, and half of it is in darkness. It is day on the lit half of Earth. It is night on the dark half of Earth. Day changes to night as Earth turns.

Sun

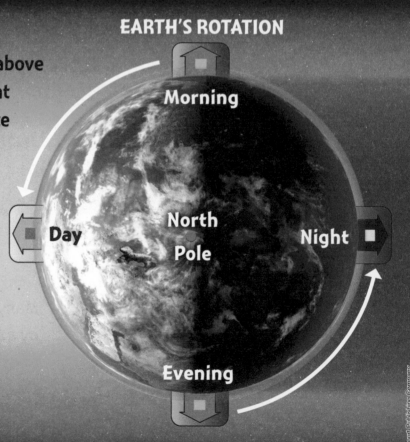

EARTH'S ROTATION

Morning

Day

North Pole

Night

Evening

Picture a line going through Earth from the North Pole to the South Pole. This imaginary line is Earth's **axis**.

Like a wheel on a bike, Earth rotates, or turns, on its axis. Earth's **rotation** [ro•TAY•shuhn] causes the cycle of day and night. One full rotation takes 24 hours, or one full day.

From one sunrise to the next, we spin through the parts of a day—morning, daytime, evening, and night. The day-night cycle happens over and over again. Think about the things you do in each part of this cycle. When do you wake up? Eat? Sleep? People follow a cycle, too!

What Time Is It?

Label each picture to show all four parts of the day-night cycle. Number the parts to show the correct sequence.

(1) morning

___ _____

___ _____

___ _____

Reasons for Seasons

spring

Winter, spring, summer, fall. Like day and night, the seasons make a cycle.

Active Reading As you read these two pages, find and underline the definition of *revolution*.

As Earth turns on its axis, it also moves around the sun. Each complete trip of Earth around the sun is one **revolution** [reh•vuh•LOO•shuhn]. Each revolution takes about 365 days, or one year.

The seasons change as Earth moves around the sun. The diagram shows that Earth is tilted on its axis. The part of Earth that points toward the sun gets more direct sunlight. The part that points away from the sun gets less. As Earth moves around the sun, the part that gets more direct sunlight changes. The part with the most direct sunlight has summer. The part with the least direct sunlight has winter. During fall and spring, neither the top nor the bottom half of Earth is tilted toward or away from the sun.

summer

Look at the image labeled *summer*. When the North Pole is pointing toward the sun, people who live north of the equator—in the Northern Hemisphere—have summer. Those in the Southern Hemisphere have winter.

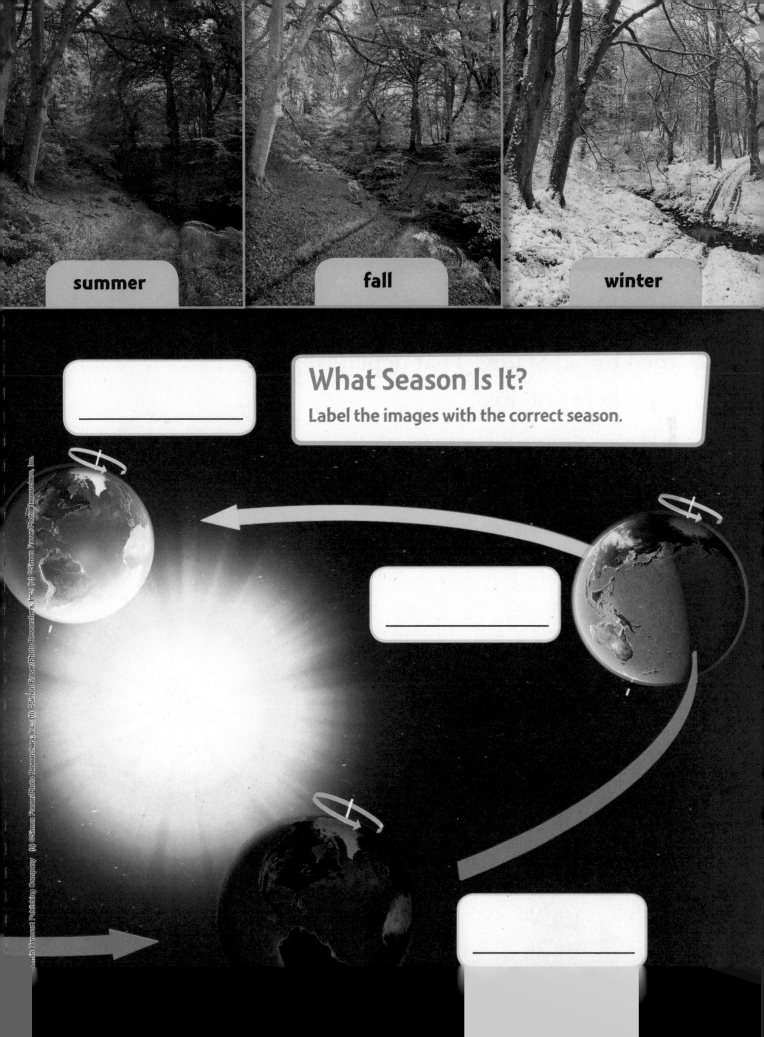

summer

fall

winter

What Season Is It?

Label the images with the correct season.

_____

_____

_____

Winter Days!

What is winter like for kids in the United States? That depends on where you live!

In Phoenix, Arizona, winter temperatures are usually in the 60s or 70s. In Portland, Oregon, they are usually in the 40s or 50s. But someone in Madison, Wisconsin, would be used to temperatures in the 20s or 30s!

In the Northeast, a big snowstorm can bring everything to a stop!

In the South, winter is usually sunny and warm. But even there, it may get cold at times!

In the Midwest, heavy snow, ice, sleet, and freezing rain are possible. Freezing rain can cause a lot of damage.

Do the Math!

Use a Data Table

Use the table to answer the questions below.

High Temperature In January			
Detroit	San Diego	Seattle	Washington, D.C.
31 °F	66 °F	47 °F	42 °F

How much warmer is San Diego than Detroit in January? _____

Which city has the coldest temperature in January? _____

Phases of the Moon

On some nights you see a round moon.
On other nights you see a sliver of moon.
Sometimes you see no moon at all. Why?

Active Reading As you study the diagram on the next page, number the moon phases to show their sequence. Begin with the new moon. Write your answers in the caption boxes.

Does moonlight really come from the moon? No! The moon doesn't produce its own light. It reflects light from the sun. This reflected light is what we see from Earth. At any time, half of the moon is lit by the sun.

As the moon revolves around Earth, different amounts of its lit side can be seen. This is what causes the different shapes, or phases, of the moon. Eight moon phases make up one cycle. A full cycle happens in about one month. Then the cycle repeats.

The Big Four Phases

The four main moon phases are new moon, full moon, and both quarter moons. Label the missing phase below. Then fill in the dark part of the moon. Use the diagram at right to help you.

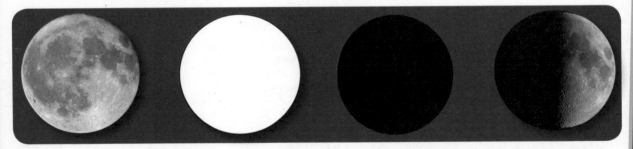

full moon   _____   new moon   first-quarter moon

up a cycle that repeats each month.

The lit side of a new moon faces away from Earth. We see no moon at all.

We see crescent moons just before and just after a new moon.

Moon Phases

During a crescent moon, just the edge of the lit side can be seen.

A third-quarter moon looks like a half-circle, but it is lit on the left side.

A first-quarter moon looks like a half-circle and is lit on the right side.

As we see less of the moon's lit side, we say that the moon is *waning*.

As we see more of the moon's lit side, we say that the moon is *waxing*.

We see all of the moon's lit side during a full moon.

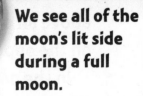

Daily Highs and Lows

Both pictures show the same beach. Why is the water so low in one picture and so high in the other? It's because of tides.

Active Reading As you read these two pages, draw boxes around the names of the two things that are being compared.

These people enjoy walking along the beach near this structure during low tide.

Tides are changes in the height of ocean water. The pull of the moon's gravity causes ocean tides. When the moon is above an ocean, it causes high tide on that part of Earth and on the opposite side, too.

In the parts of the ocean between the two areas of high tide, the water level is lower. At those places, a low tide occurs.

Pattern of Tides

On the lines below, tell where the moon might have been when the picture on this page was taken.

_____

_____

_____

_____

_____

In the space below, draw what the image on this page will look like next as it continues its cycle.

Where have all the people gone? They didn't want to get wet! They left before it was high tide.

At most beaches, there are high tides and low tides every day. The tides make a cycle. How do you know it is high tide here now? Before, we saw people walking on the beach. Now, the beach is covered with water!

Sum It Up!

When you're done, use the answer key to check and revise your work.

Finish each statement. Then draw a line from the statement to the picture that matches it.

1 Each month the moon cycles through eight _____.

2 Earth's _____ causes the cycle of day and night.

3 When the North Pole tilts away from the sun, it is this _____ in Earth's northern half.

4 At low _____, you can find seashells on the beach.

5 Earth makes one _____ in about one year.

6 The Earth is tilted to one side on its _____.

A

B

C

D

E

F

336

Answer Key: 1. F, phases **2.** A, rotation **3.** D, season **4.** C, tide **5.** B, revolution **6.** E, axis

Name _____

Word Play

1 Unscramble each word to complete the sentence. Write it in the boxes.

1. h e s a p

We see different shapes of light in each _____ of the moon.

⬜⬜⬜⬜⬜

2. d i s e t

The pull of the moon on Earth's oceans results in _____.

⬜⬜⬜⬜⬜

3. i n o t r v e u l o

It takes Earth a year to make one complete _____.

⬜⬜⬜⬜⬜⬜⬜⬜⬜

4. o a n o t t r i

Earth's _____ causes the cycle of day and night.

⬜⬜⬜⬜⬜⬜⬜⬜

5. x a s i

Earth's _____ passes through the North and South Poles.

⬜⬜⬜⬜

6. p i n n s i g n

Earth's _____ , or rotating, causes day and night.

⬜⬜⬜⬜⬜⬜⬜⬜

Write the circled letters here. Unscramble them to form a word that answers the riddle.

___ ___ ___ ___ ___ ___

7. In this season, plants begin to grow.

⬜⬜⬜⬜⬜⬜

Apply Concepts

2 Put a circle around the image of Earth that shows winter in the Northern Hemisphere. Put an X on the image that shows summer in the Southern Hemisphere. Put squares around the images that show spring and fall.

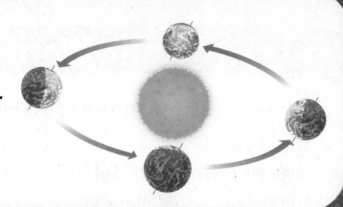

3 Explain how Earth is moving. Tell what cycle this motion causes.

_____

_____

_____

_____

4 Draw and label pictures to show the four main phases of the moon in order.

_____ _____ _____ _____

Take It Home!

Go outside with your family on a clear night. Tell your family what phase the moon is in now. Tell them what phase it will enter next. Explain how you know.

Meet the Space Scientists

Katherine Johnson 1918–

Katherine Johnson was a "human computer" at NASA. With her knowledge of math, she helped astronauts travel into space. Johnson computed the path the spacecrafts would take. In 1961, she figured out the flight path for the first American in space, Alan Shepard. By 1962, NASA was using real computers for John Glenn's orbits around Earth. But they still called on Johnson to check the computers' numbers.

In 1969, Johnson worked to help the *Apollo 11* spacecraft travel into space. During this trip, Neil Armstrong became the first human to walk on the moon.

Amanda Nahm

Amanda Nahm is a planetary scientist. She studies the surfaces of planets and the moon. When a meteoroid hits the surface of a planet or moon, it forms a crater, or hole. The craters on the moon have been there for billions of years. Larger craters often have cracks, or faults, that form around them. By studying these craters and faults, Nahm can learn about the history of the moon's formation.

Nahm studies the Orientale Basin—the youngest impact crater on the moon. An arrow points to the young crater.

Moon Mission

Katherine Johnson and Amanda Nahm study space in different ways. Write the name of the correct scientist below each statement.

1 I study impact craters on the surface of the moon.

_____

2 I computed the flight path to the moon.

_____

3 I worked for NASA for many years.

_____

4 I want to learn about the history of the moon's formation.

_____

Name _____

Essential Question

How Can We Model the Moon's Phases?

Set a Purpose
What will you learn from this modeling activity?

_____

_____

_____

Think About the Procedure
Why does only one person move?

_____

_____

_____

Why is the student in the center drawing the moon?

_____

_____

_____

Record Your Observations
Add shading to the circles to show the part of the moon's surface that is dark. Label each moon phase.

Position 1

◯

_____

Position 2

◯

_____

Position 3

◯

_____

Position 4

◯

_____

Draw Conclusions

How did the model help you understand why the moon's phases occur?

_____

_____

_____

_____

Analyze and Extend

1. Why does the moon appear to change when viewed from Earth?

_____

_____

_____

_____

2. During a full moon, is the whole moon lit? Explain.

_____

_____

_____

_____

3. If you were on the sun, would the moon look the same as it does from Earth? Explain.

_____

_____

_____

_____

4. Where would the student holding the ball stand to model a crescent moon? How do you know?

_____

_____

_____

_____

5. What other questions do you have about the phases of the moon?

_____

_____

_____

_____

How It Works:
Keck Observatory

An observatory is a kind of system. It has many parts that work together. Scientists use observatories to study space. Read about the parts of the Keck Observatory in Hawaii.

The Keck Observatory has two telescopes. Both are as tall as eight-story buildings!

The dome protects the telescope's mirrors from rain and sunlight.

An opening in the dome turns to show different areas of the sky.

The 10-meter main mirror is a powerful magnifier. It is made up of smaller mirrors.

Can You Fix It?

Each part of a system plays a role. If one part breaks, the system may not work. The picture below shows the telescope's main mirror.

This planet was photographed by the Keck Observatory.

Trace the path of the light through the telescope by following the red arrows in the image below.

What would happen if one part of the mirror broke? How could you fix the telescope if this happened?

_____

_____

_____

Build On It!

Rise to the engineering design challenge—complete **Owner's Manual: Using a Telescope** on the Inquiry Flipchart.

Name _____

Vocabulary Review

Use the terms in the box to complete the sentences.

> axis
> revolution
> rotation
> tide

1. Earth takes 24 hours to complete one full _____.

2. Earth changes from season to season as it continues its trip around the sun, which is called a(n) _____.

3. The way the moon's gravity changes the height of the ocean is known as the _____.

4. The seasons on Earth change because of the tilt of Earth's _____.

Science Concepts

Fill in the letter of the choice that best answers the question.

5. Misha spends much of his time at the beach. He collects shells. If he gets there too late, the ocean water covers the shells. What is happening at Misha's beach while he collects shells?

   Ⓐ The moon is above the ocean at his beach.

   Ⓑ Water is falling downhill onto the shells.

   Ⓒ The tide is low when he looks for shells.

   Ⓓ The moon's gravity is pushing the ocean onto the beach.

6. Mae's family is meeting in Montana for a reunion. Mae learned in school that winters in Montana are cold and snowy. She also learned that Montana is farther north than many other states. What is the main reason Montana has such cold winters?

   Ⓐ Montana is closer to the sun than other states.

   Ⓑ Montana is covered by clouds in the winter.

   Ⓒ Montana gets too much direct sunlight in the winter.

   Ⓓ Montana does not get much direct sunlight in the winter.

Science Concepts

Fill in the letter of the choice that best answers the question.

7. Mr. Perez's students are learning about the phases of the moon. They made this sequence in a model to show the phases the moon goes through over a two-week period.

Which statement best describes the changes in the moon's phases during this time?

Ⓐ The moon is waxing from a new moon to a full moon.

Ⓑ The moon is waning from a new moon to a full moon.

Ⓒ The moon is waxing from a full moon to a new moon.

Ⓓ The moon is waning from a full moon to a new moon.

8. Earth's relationship to the sun influences the length of our days. Which **best** explains this relationship?

Ⓐ Earth revolves around the sun every 24 hours.

Ⓑ The sun revolves around Earth every 24 hours.

Ⓒ The sun shines on Earth for 12 hours each day.

Ⓓ Earth rotates on its axis with part of Earth getting sunlight.

9. Sara asked her parents why we have four seasons. She already understood that one of the poles is tilted toward the sun during summer and winter. Sara is confused about spring and fall. How did her parents explain these seasons?

Ⓐ The poles are less tilted toward or away from the sun during these seasons.

Ⓑ Both the top and bottom halves of Earth are tilted toward the sun.

Ⓒ Earth stops revolving around the sun during spring and fall.

Ⓓ Earth rotates away from the sun for two seasons during the year.

10. The diagram below shows Earth's rotation on its axis. It also shows Earth's revolution around the sun.

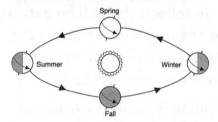

What changes in this diagram during Earth's rotation and revolution?

Ⓐ The sun begins to revolve around Earth.

Ⓑ The part of Earth tilted toward the sun changes.

Ⓒ Earth changes the direction of its rotation on its axis.

Ⓓ Earth changes the direction of its revolution around the sun.

11. Sunset Elementary's third graders visited a nearby beach on a field trip. Before they left, they studied the times of high and low tide. They wanted to get to the beach during low tide. The picture below shows what the beach looked like when they arrived.

In this picture, what shows that they arrived at low tide?

Ⓐ The waves are hitting away from the dunes.

Ⓑ The waves are hitting the dunes.

Ⓒ Sand covers much of the beach.

Ⓓ Water covers much of the beach.

12. The moon has different phases. What is different between a first-quarter moon and a third-quarter moon?

Ⓐ their shapes

Ⓑ the side of the moon that appears lit

Ⓒ their sizes

Ⓓ the side of Earth that appears lit

13. Piper wanted to learn more about the moon. She borrowed a book about the moon from her library. Each night at dinner, she shared what she was learning with members of her family. One night, she told them that the moon's gravity influences Earth's natural cycles. How do you think she explained this?

Ⓐ We see the moon's light and shape each night.

Ⓑ The moon causes Earth's day-night cycle.

Ⓒ When we see a new moon, we see half of the moon.

Ⓓ When the moon is over an ocean, it causes high tide.

14. When the sun rises each morning, a new cycle begins. What happens at the beginning of this cycle?

Ⓐ The moon's gravity pulls the sun's light toward Earth.

Ⓑ The moon begins its revolution around Earth again.

Ⓒ Earth begins its revolution around the sun again.

Ⓓ Earth's rotation continues the day-night cycle.

Apply Inquiry and Review the Big Idea

Write the answers to these questions.

15. The lifeguards at a local beach record the tides each day. The chart below shows the high and low tides over two days.

Tides for December		
Day	Tides	Time
4	low	12:13 A.M.
	high	5:20 A.M.
	low	12:40 P.M.
	high	7:21 P.M.
5	low	1:32 A.M.
	high	6:55 A.M.
	low	1:35 P.M.
	high	8:02 P.M.

Write two comparisons about the tides over two days.

_____

_____

_____

The following chart is a record of the four main phases of the moon over a four-month period. Use this chart to answer questions 16 and 17.

Moon Phases—Summer 2005				
Month	New moon	First quarter	Full moon	Third quarter
June	6	15	22	28
July	6	14	21	28
August	5	13	19	26
September	4	11	18	25

16. During which two periods in July and the first part of August could you see a crescent moon?

_____

17. Use the chart to estimate the dates for each moon phase for October and November.

October _____

November _____

Matter

© Houghton Mifflin Harcourt Publishing Company (bg) ©Jeff Hunter/The Image Bank/Getty Images (inset) ©Comstock/Getty Images (border) ©NDisc/Age Fotostock

Big Idea

Matter has properties that can be observed, described, and measured. Matter can change.

coral reef in
Key Largo, Florida

I Wonder Why

The colors of coral and fish can help us learn how to use properties of matter. Why is this so? *Turn the page to find out.*

Here's why Color is a physical property of matter. You can use color to sort coral and fish into groups.

In this unit, you will explore the Big Idea, the Essential Questions, and the Investigations on the Inquiry Flipchart.

Track Your Progress

Levels of Inquiry Key ■ DIRECTED ■ GUIDED ■ INDEPENDENT

Big Idea Matter has properties that can be observed, described, and measured. Matter can change.

Essential Questions

Now I Get the Big Idea!

Science Notebook
Before you begin each lesson, be sure to write your thoughts about the Essential Question.

Essential Question

What Are Some Physical Properties?

Engage Your Brain!

Find the answer to the question in this lesson and record it here.

How can you compare these beach umbrellas?

_____

_____

_____

Active Reading

Lesson Vocabulary

List the terms, and make notes in the Interactive Glossary as you learn more.

_____

_____

_____

_____

Compare and Contrast

Many ideas in this lesson are connected because they explain comparisons and contrasts—how things are alike and different. Active readers stay focused on comparisons and contrasts when they ask themselves, How are things alike? How are they different?

It's Everything!

What is matter? Everything you see on this page is matter. All the "stuff" around you is matter.

Active Reading As you read the next page, draw a line under each main idea.

Texture is the way something feels. Objects can be smooth or rough. What is the texture of sand?

_____

_____

Matter can be different colors. Write a sentence that describes the color of the beach ball.

_____

_____

Matter is anything that takes up space. Your science book takes up more space than your pencil does. Did you know that no two things can take up the same space?

You describe matter by naming its physical properties. A **physical property** is a characteristic of matter that you can observe or measure directly. Look in the boxes to learn about some properties of matter.

Even we are made of matter!

Hardness describes how easily an object's shape can be changed. Name a hard object you see.

_____

_____

_____

_____

Size is how big something is. Which object is the biggest? Which one takes up the most space?

_____

_____

Shape is the form an object has. What words can you use to describe the two smallest shells?

_____

_____

_____

How Much Mass?

Why is it so difficult to lift a bucket full of water? Would it be easier to carry the water in smaller containers instead?

Active Reading As you read these two pages, find and underline the definition of *mass*. Then circle the name of the tool we use to measure mass.

Mass is the amount of matter an object has. Mass is also a measure of how hard it is to move an object. The more mass an object has, the harder it is to move the object.

How can you measure the mass of sand, water, or other materials in a bucket? Check out the next page.

Measure It!

We use a pan balance to measure mass. The pan balance measures mass in grams (g). How can you measure the mass of the contents of a bucket? To find the mass, you have to use math.

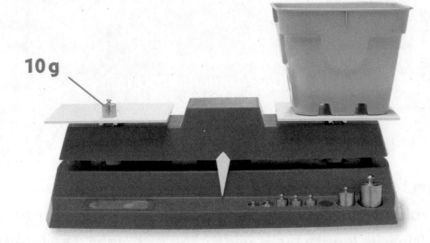

Find the mass of the container alone. _____

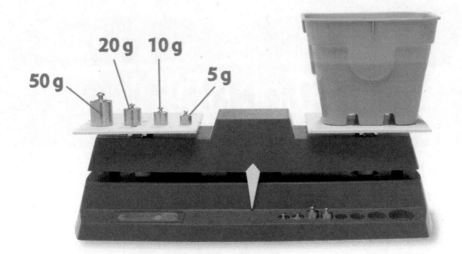

Find the mass of the container + contents. _____

Now you subtract to find the mass of the contents.

Mass of the container + contents	−	Mass of the container	=	Mass of the contents
_____		_____		_____

What's the Volume?

Matter takes up space. How can you measure the amount of space an object takes up?

Active Reading As you read the next page, circle the name of a tool you can use to measure volume. Underline the units it uses.

An object's **volume** is the amount of space it takes up. To find the volume of a cube or a rectangular [rek•TAN•gyuh•luhr] solid, multiply its length by its width and its height. The length, width, and height of the small cube below are one centimeter.

Do the Math!
Find the Volume

This cube's volume is one cubic centimeter.

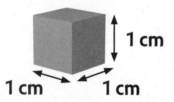

1 cm
1 cm   1 cm

Find the volume of this cube.

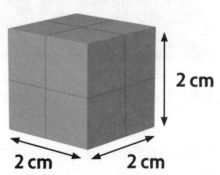

2 cm
2 cm   2 cm

_____ x _____ x _____ = _____ cubic centimeters
  L   W   H

Use a graduated cylinder to measure the volume of a liquid. The units are in milliliters (mL). You can also use it to find the volume of a solid.

Measure It!

Read the level of the water in the graduated cylinder. This is the volume of the water.

_____

Add a shell and read the volume again. This is the volume of the water + the shell.

_____

Now subtract to find the volume of the shell. The volume of a solid is measured in cubic centimeters. 1 milliliter equals 1 cubic centimeter, so just change *milliliters* to *cubic centimeters.*

volume of water + shell   volume of water   volume of shell

_____ - _____ = _____

Hot and Cold

At the beach, you can feel the difference between hot sand and cold water. How do you measure how warm something is?

Active Reading As you read this page, circle the names of the temperature scales that are being compared.

Temperature is a measure of how warm something is. You use a thermometer to measure temperature.

Thermometers use a scale of numbers to show temperature. There are two scales that are frequently used.

Most weather reports use the Fahrenheit [FAIR•uhn•hyt] scale. On this scale, water becomes ice at 32 degrees. Water boils at 212 degrees.

The other scale is the Celsius [SEL•see•uhs] scale. On this scale, water becomes ice at 0 degrees. Water boils at 100 degrees.

> What temperature does the thermometer show?
>
> _____
>
> _____

Measure It!

Write the air temperature and water temperature on the lines. Then color the thermometer to show the temperature of the sand.

Air Temperature

_____ degrees Celsius

_____ degrees Fahrenheit

You can feel the sand's higher temperature and the water's lower temperature.

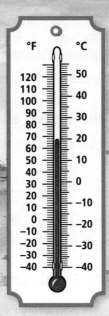

Water Temperature

_____ degrees Celsius

_____ degrees Fahrenheit

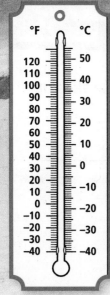

Sand Temperature

The sand's temperature is 37 degrees Celsius. Show that temperature on the thermometer.

Sum It Up!

When you're done, use the answer key to check and revise your work.

Write the vocabulary term that matches the picture and caption.

1

This crab takes up space and has mass.

_____

2

The blue color is a characteristic of the kite.

_____

3

This manatee has a large amount of matter.

_____

4

This umbrella takes up a lot of space.

_____

5

This thermometer tells how hot it is today.

_____

Answer Key: 1. matter 2. physical property 3. mass 4. volume 5. temperature

Name _____

Word Play

1 Write four words from the box to complete this word web about the physical properties of matter.

| mass | volume | thermometer | color | milliliters | temperature |

_____

_____

Physical Properties

_____

_____

Apply Concepts

In questions 2–4, write the name of the measurement tool you would use.

 2 Degrees Celsius   **3** Milliliters   **4** Grams

Is one drink colder than the other?

Which cup holds the most liquid?

Does a glass of milk have more matter than a glass of punch?

_____   _____   _____

5 Choose an object in your classroom. Write as many physical properties as you can to describe it.

_____

_____

_____

Take It Home! Share what you have learned about properties of matter with your family. With a family member, name properties of matter at mealtime or in places in your home.

Ask a Metallurgist

gold bars

aluminum foil

Now It's Your Turn!

What properties make steel a good material to use for building bridges?

_____

_____

_____

Q. What is a metallurgist?

A. A metallurgist is a scientist who works with metals. Iron, aluminum, gold, and copper are just some of these metals. They also combine different metals to make a new metal.

Q. Why do they combine different metals?

A. Metals may have different weights, strengths, and hardnesses. They combine metals to change their properties. The new metal may be stronger, harder, or a different color.

Q. How do they use the properties of metals in their work?

A. They look at the properties of metals and how metals can be used. Iron is strong. Mixed with other materials it becomes steel. Steel is a hard and strong metal. Copper can conduct electricity. It's a good metal to use for electrical wires.

copper pennies

This Leads to That

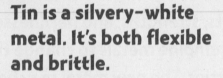

Copper is a soft, red metal. It can be shaped into things and over time turns green.

Tin is a silvery-white metal. It's both flexible and brittle.

Bronze is made by mixing tin and copper. The gold metal is hard and strong. Over time bronze turns green.

Compare the properties of copper and bronze. Then complete the table.

Properties of copper	Properties of both	Properties of bronze

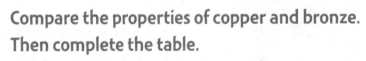

Bronze is shaped to make sculptures and bells.

Essential Question

What Are the States of Matter?

Find the answer to the following question in this lesson and record it here.

How does heating this frozen treat affect it?

_____

_____

 Active Reading

Lesson Vocabulary
List the terms, and make notes in the Interactive Glossary as you learn more.

_____

_____

_____

_____

_____

Signal Words: Cause and Effect
Signal words show connections between ideas. Words signaling a cause include *because* and *if*. Words signaling an effect include *so* and *thus*. Active readers remember what they read because they are alert to signal words that identify causes and effects.

What's the State?

What a party! You can eat a piece of solid cake, drink a cold liquid, or play with a gas-filled balloon.

Active Reading As you read these two pages, draw circles around the names of the three states of matter that are being compared.

There are three common states of matter. They are solid, liquid, and gas. Water can be found in all three states.

A **solid** is matter that takes up a definite amount of space. A solid also has a definite shape. Your science book is a solid. Ice is also a solid.

A **liquid** is matter that also takes up a definite amount of space, but it does not have a definite shape. Liquids take the shape of their containers. Drinking water is a liquid.

A **gas** is matter that does not take up a definite amount of space and does not have a definite shape. The air around you is a gas.

curtains _____

ribbon _____

ice cubes _____

orange drink _____

▶ Identify the solids, liquids, and gases in the picture by writing *S, L,* or *G* in each box.

air in balloon _____

bubbles _____

plastic _____

Cool! It's Freezing!

Water freezes at 0 °C.

When matter cools, it loses energy. How does cooling affect water?

Active Reading As you read these two pages, draw circles around the clue words that signal a cause-and-effect relationship.

All the pictures show water at a temperature lower than 0 degrees Celsius (0 °C) or 32 degrees Fahrenheit (32 °F). How do we know this? If liquid water cools to that temperature, it freezes. Below that temperature, water exists as a solid—ice. Freezing is the change of state from a liquid to a solid.

How would this igloo be different if its temperature was 10 °C?

_____

_____

How can you tell that the temperature of the snow is below 0 °C?

_____

_____

Hail is water that falls to Earth as small balls of ice.

This snowball holds together because the water in it is frozen into a solid.

This girl can skate on ice because ice is a solid.

Do the Math!
Solve a Story Problem

The temperature of a puddle of water is 10 °C. The water cools by two degrees every hour. In how many hours will the puddle of water begin to freeze? Explain how you got your answer.

_____

_____

_____

_____

_____

Just Add Heat!

When matter is heated, it gains energy. How can heating affect water?

Water is a liquid between the temperatures of 0 °C and 100 °C.

If the sun heats this ice sculpture enough, it will begin to melt.

What happens to an ice cube after you take it from the freezer? As it warms, it begins to melt. Melting is the change of state from a solid to a liquid. Ice melts at the same temperature that liquid water freezes—0 °C (32 °F). Melting is the opposite of freezing.

If you heat a pot of water on the stove, the temperature of the water increases until it reaches 100 °C (212 °F). At 100 °C, water boils, or changes rapidly to a gas called *water vapor*. You can't see water vapor. It's invisible.

Water boils at 100 °C.

What's the Temperature?

Draw a line from each thermometer to the picture that shows the state of water indicated by the temperature on the thermometer.

garden hose

ice cube

boiling water

Now You See It...

Liquid water can change to a gas without boiling. Look at the drawings of a puddle. What changes do you see?

Water can evaporate at temperatures below 100°C.

Active Reading As you read these two pages, draw a line under each main idea.

Liquid water does not have to boil to become a gas. When you sweat on a hot day, the water on your skin disappears. The liquid water turns into a gas. This is called **evaporation** [ee•vap•uh•RAY•shuhn]. Water can evaporate from other places, such as a puddle.

The sun's heat makes the water in the puddle change to water vapor, which goes into the air.

The puddle gets smaller as the water disappears. Most of the liquid water has changed to a gas.

A gas can change back to a liquid. This is called **condensation** [kahn•duhn•SAY•shuhn]. Water vapor condenses as it cools and loses energy. Water vapor in the air condenses on a cold car window. The outside of a cold soft drink can becomes wet on a hot day. The grass on a cool morning may have dew on it. These are all condensation.

▶ What happened to water vapor in this girl's warm breath as she breathed on the cold window?

_____

_____

_____

Sum It Up!

When you're done, use the answer key to check and revise your work.

Read the statements. Then draw a line to match each statement with the correct picture.

1 This state of matter does not have a definite size or shape.

A

2 This state of matter has a definite size and takes the shape of its container.

B

3 During this process, a liquid changes to a gas.

C

4 This state of matter has a definite size and shape.

D

5 During this process, a gas changes to a liquid.

E

Answer Key: 1. E, 2. B, 3. A, 4. C, 5. D

Name _____

Word Play

1 Use the words in the box to complete the puzzle.

solid*   liquid*   gas*   evaporation*   condensation*

*Key Lesson Vocabulary

Across

2. Boiling changes liquid water to this state.

4. At 0 °C, ice can change to this state if heat is added.

5. The water in a puddle changes to a gas through this process.

Down

1. A gas changes to a liquid through this process.

3. Ice is water in this state.

Apply Concepts

2 Make a list of solids, liquids, and gases in your school.

_____

_____

_____

3 Think about what happens to a glass of cold water outside on a hot day. Use the words *evaporation* and *condensation* to describe what happens to the water inside the glass and what happens on the outside of the glass.

_____

_____

_____

_____

4 Which picture shows solid water? Which shows liquid water? Label the pictures.

_____   _____

Take It Home!

Share what you have learned about the states of matter with your family. With a family member, name states of matter that are present at mealtime or in places in your home.

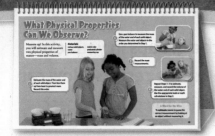

Name _____

© Houghton Mifflin Harcourt Publishing Company

Essential Question

What Physical Properties Can We Observe?

Set a Purpose

What skills will you use in this activity?

_____

_____

Think About the Procedure

How can you estimate the masses of the objects and water to place them in order?

_____

_____

_____

How can you estimate the volumes of the objects and water to place them in order?

_____

_____

Record Your Data

List the objects and water in the order you placed them when you estimated their masses and volumes. Then record their actual measurements.

Mass	
Object	Measurement

Volume	
Object	Measurement

Draw Conclusions

When you used water to find the volume of one or more of the objects, why did the volume of the water have to be greater than the volume of the object?

_____

_____

_____

_____

Analyze and Extend

1. Were your estimates correct? Why?

_____

_____

_____

_____

2. Suppose you have two cubes. They are made of the same material, but one has a greater volume than the other. Does the larger cube have more mass? Explain your answer.

_____

_____

_____

_____

3. Did all the groups in your class have the same results? How can you explain any differences?

_____

_____

_____

_____

_____

_____

_____

_____

4. When would you have to use a measuring cup to find the volume of a solid?

_____

_____

_____

_____

5. Think of another question you would like to ask about measuring mass and volume.

_____

_____

_____

_____

Essential Question

What Are Some Changes to Matter?

Engage Your Brain!

Find the answer to the following question in this lesson and record it here.

How have these foods been changed to make a salad?

_____

_____

_____

Active Reading

Lesson Vocabulary

List the terms. As you learn about each one, make notes in the Interactive Glossary.

_____ _____

_____ _____

_____

Compare and Contrast

Many ideas in this lesson are connected because they explain comparisons and contrasts—how things are alike and different. Active readers stay focused on comparisons and contrasts when they ask themselves, How are these things alike? How are they different?

Physical Changes

A change to matter can be either physical or chemical. In physical changes, substances keep their identity. No new matter is formed.

Active Reading As you read these two pages, underline examples of physical changes.

A firefighter folds a piece of paper in half. She tears along the fold. Then she cuts out the shape of a truck.

Two physical properties have changed: size and shape. The cut-out truck is still paper. The scraps are still paper. In a **physical change**, the kind of matter stays the same. Folding, tearing, and cutting are all physical changes.

Many objects are made of one or more kinds of matter. A fire hose contains rubber and fabric. Cutting, bending, and shaping these materials to make the hose are all physical changes. The shapes and sizes of the materials have changed, but they are still the same materials.

Inside a fire hose

Make a Change!

Draw two pictures that show a hose before and after a physical change. Label your pictures to tell how the hose was changed.

MOUNT DORA

MOUNT DORA
FIRE/RESCUE

The firefighter's sponge is torn. The big piece is a sponge. The little piece is also a sponge. The kind of matter stayed the same. A physical change took place.

Mixtures and Solutions

Yum! Cool lemonade tastes good in a hot firehouse. Several kinds of matter make lemonade a tasty mixture.

Active Reading As you read these two pages, find an example of a solution. Circle the word that names the solution and the picture that shows it.

Fruit salad is a mixture. A **mixture** is two or more substances that are combined without changing any of them. Because no new matter is formed, making a mixture is a physical change.

A box of paints and markers is a mixture. So is a chest of toys. Can you name another mixture?

Many different kinds of fruit have been cut and put into the bowl. Each kind of fruit in this mixture has kept its identity.

A **solution** [suh•LOO•shuhn] is a mixture in which all the substances are evenly mixed. Salt water is a solution. So is tea. To make a solution, you completely mix, or **dissolve**, one substance in another.

All solutions are mixtures. Lemonade is a mixture of water, sugar, and lemon juice. It is also a solution because the sugar and lemon juice have dissolved in the water.

Each kind of matter in a solution keeps its identity. It may not seem that way because you cannot see all the different substances. All their tiniest parts are evenly mixed together.

What's In It?

Complete each sentence.

1. Lemonade is one kind of _____.

2. To make lemonade, you _____ sugar and lemon juice in water.

3. In a _____ like lemonade, substances are evenly mixed together.

Properties Matter!

You can separate a mixture using its properties.

Active Reading As you read this page, draw two lines under the main idea.

Blueberries remain blueberries when you put them in a salad. Sugar is still sugar when you stir it into tea. Each kind of matter keeps its identity. Because making a mixture is a physical change, you can separate a mixture using the physical properties of its parts.

The firefighters' boat and the rescue ring float. Floating is a physical property. You can use it to separate some mixtures. Just add water, and scoop off the objects that float.

Matter that is smaller than the holes passes through the sieve [SIV]. Matter that is larger than the holes stays on top.

A magnet picks up matter that contains iron. This giant magnet separates iron from plastic and other materials in a junkyard.

As the sun heats this saltwater lake, the water evaporates. The salt is left behind. The salt and the water have been separated.

Take It Apart

How could you separate each of the mixtures below?

_____

_____

_____

_____

_____

_____

Chemical Changes

Can you unmix a fruit salad? Sure. Can you uncook an egg? No! How does an egg change when you cook it?

Active Reading As you read these two pages, draw boxes around the two kinds of changes that are being compared.

Uh oh. Someone forgot to clean up after a picnic. Fresh fruit and hardboiled eggs were left in the sun. The bananas have turned black. The strawberries are covered in white fuzz. The eggs are rotting—and they stink!

Chemical changes have taken place in the foods. How are chemical changes different from physical changes? In a **chemical change**, new kinds of matter are formed. Some chemical changes can be reversed using chemical means. But most of the chemical changes you see, such as the changes to food mentioned above, cannot be reversed.

A new mailbox is made from strong metal. Over time, metal can rust. It changes color and becomes weaker. These are signs of a chemical change.

Chemical changes happen all around you. They cause the green leaves on some trees to turn red, orange, and yellow. After the leaves fall, they begin to decompose, or break down, forming new kinds of matter.

Chemical changes happen in your body. After a scraped knee stops bleeding, a scab begins to form. The scab is a new kind of matter. Suppose you eat a pear. As your body digests the pear, chemical changes break it up into simpler substances that your body can use.

Wood burns. New kinds of matter—smoke, ash, and charcoal—are formed.

What's Cooking?

Your dad fries an egg. That's a chemical change. Name one more chemical change you could see at breakfast. How can you tell it's a chemical change?

_____

_____

_____

_____

This small fire burns off wood and leaves, which could fuel a big fire. The firefighter sprays water on the flames. He controls the burn to keep the fire from causing harm.

Making Bagels

Wow, take a look inside this kitchen! It's filled with changes in matter as bagels are made. Hands and kitchen tools cause physical changes. Yeast and heat cause chemical changes.

1 The bakers put yeast, sugar, and flour in warm water to make dough. This causes a chemical change. Then they shape the dough into rings. That's a physical change.

2 Plop! Heat from the boiling water causes the yeast to give off a gas. This makes the bagels puff up. The water changes the crust and makes it chewy!

3 What's your favorite kind of bagel? Adding a tasty topping like these sesame [SES•uh•mee] seeds is a physical change.

Do the Math!
Solve a Two-Step Problem

You can make 100 bagels with 10 pounds of flour. How many bagels can you make with 20 pounds of flour? Show your work.

_____

_____

_____

_____

4 Can you unbake a bagel and get back the original ingredients? No! Their identities have changed.

Sum It Up!

When you're done, use the answer key to check and revise your work.

Fill in the blank in each sentence. Then draw a line to the matching picture.

1 Tearing an object is a _____ change.

2 You cannot see the individual _____ in a solution.

3 The parts of a saltwater solution can be _____.

4 Foods undergo _____ changes as they cook.

5 When you make a salad, the physical _____ of the ingredients stay the same.

Answer Key: 1. physical; sponge 2. substances; lemonade 3. separated; lake 4. chemical; bagels 5. properties; salad

Word Play

Underline the correct meaning or description of each term.

1 physical change
- a change in which the type of matter stays the same
- a change in which nothing is different
- a change in which a new kind of matter is formed

2 mixture
- substances are cooked
- substances keep their identities
- substances can't be separated

3 solution
- some parts float
- parts are evenly mixed
- parts are unevenly mixed

4 dissolve
- become unmixed
- become evenly mixed
- become unevenly mixed

5 chemical change
- matter is cut into smaller pieces
- matter is neatly folded
- new kinds of matter are formed

Apply Concepts

6 Tell whether each picture below shows a physical change or a chemical change and explain how you know.

_____

_____

_____

_____

_____

_____

_____

_____

_____

_____

7 Look at the mixture below. Explain how you could separate it.

_____

_____

_____

_____

_____

Take It Home! Share with your family what you have learned about changes in matter. With a family member, name changes in matter that you observe at mealtimes in your home.

Name _____

Essential Question

What Changes Can We Observe?

Set a Purpose
What will you learn from this experiment?

_____

_____

Think About the Procedure
Why do you think you use equal amounts of water and vinegar and equal amounts of baking soda?

_____

_____

_____

_____

_____

_____

_____

Why are safety goggles needed to do this experiment?

_____

_____

_____

_____

Record Your Data
Record your results in the table.

My Observations	
Substances	**Observations**
Baking soda and water	_____ _____ _____
Baking soda and vinegar	_____ _____ _____

Draw Conclusions

What kind of change did you see in each cup? How do you know?

_____

_____

_____

_____

_____

_____

_____

_____

Analyze and Extend

1. In which step did you see a new kind of matter form?

_____

2. How did you know that a new kind of matter had formed?

_____

_____

_____

_____

3. Scientists sometimes compare their observations during an experiment with something that they already know or understand. Compare other things you've seen with what happened to the baking soda in water and in vinegar.

_____

_____

_____

_____

_____

4. Think of another question you would like to ask about the changes that occur when you mix one substance with another.

_____

_____

_____

_____

Resources on the Road

Machines are made using natural resources. Read about the natural resources used to make a car.

Glass is made from minerals. This glass is coated in plastic. It is hard to recycle.

Seats are cotton and plastic. Cotton comes from plants. Plastic is made from oil. Seats often end up in landfills.

Steel makes up the car's frame. Steel is a mixture of metals and can be recycled.

Tires are made from rubber and metal. Rubber comes from trees. Tires can be recycled.

Why is it important to recycle car parts?

_____

_____

_____

Change the Design

The supply of many natural resources is limited. Tell what natural resources make up the bicycle parts.

A bike helmet is a technology that uses cloth and plastic.

_____

cotton and plastic

_____

_____

Pick one part of the bicycle. Tell how you could change the design to use fewer resources.

_____

_____

Build On It!

Rise to the engineering design challenge—complete **Design It: Float Your Boat** on the Inquiry Flipchart.

Name _____

Vocabulary Review

Use the terms in the box to complete the sentences.

> volume
> liquid
> physical properties
> physical change
> evaporation
> solution

1. If you stir sugar into hot tea, the sugar will completely mix in the water, forming a _____.

2. If you multiply the length of a rectangular solid by its width and its height, you will find its _____.

3. Molding clay into the shape of an animal is an example of a _____.

4. The size and shape of an object are some of its _____.

5. At 30 °C, water is a _____.

6. Liquid water can change to a gas by boiling or by _____.

Science Concepts

Fill in the letter of the choice that best answers the question.

7. A rock has a mass of 30 g. A block also has a mass of 30 g. What must be true about the rock and the block?

  (A) They have the same volume.

  (B) They are the same temperature.

  (C) They contain the same type of matter.

  (D) They contain the same amount of matter.

8. Ari wants to find the volume of a rectangular box. What should he do to find the volume of the box?

  (A) Measure the length and height of the box. Multiply the length by the height.

  (B) Measure the length and height of the box. Add the length and the height.

  (C) Measure the length, width, and height of the box. Multiply the length by the width and the height.

  (D) Measure the length, width, and height of the box. Add the length, the width, and the height.

Science Concepts

Fill in the letter of the choice that best answers the question.

9. The picture below shows a change of state.

What state change is taking place in the picture?

Ⓐ solid to liquid

Ⓑ solid to gas

Ⓒ liquid to gas

Ⓓ liquid to solid

10. Stephanie observes the color of a liquid. Then she uses a thermometer to measure the temperature of the liquid. Finally, she uses a graduated cylinder to find the volume of the liquid. What type of properties did Stephanie observe?

Ⓐ physical properties

Ⓑ chemical properties

Ⓒ temporary properties

Ⓓ permanent properties

11. Origami is the art of paper folding. Swans, flowers, and many other shapes can be made out of colored paper. What type of change takes place in origami?

Ⓐ chemical change

Ⓑ color change

Ⓒ physical change

Ⓓ solution change

12. Darshana pours 50 mL of water into a graduated cylinder. She places a small toy dinosaur into the graduated cylinder. It sinks to the bottom. She observes that the water level rises to 63 mL. What can Darshana conclude?

Ⓐ The mass of the dinosaur is 13 mL.

Ⓑ The mass of the dinosaur is 63 mL.

Ⓒ The volume of the dinosaur is 13 mL.

Ⓓ The volume of the dinosaur is 63 mL.

13. Salih places objects on a balance. What is Salih **most likely** doing?

Ⓐ He is comparing the lengths of two objects.

Ⓑ He is comparing the masses of two objects.

Ⓒ He is comparing the hardness of two objects.

Ⓓ He is comparing the volumes of two objects.

14. Aidan and Carlos went camping. The pictures show one thing the boys did on their camping trip.

Which sentence explains how the boys knew a chemical change took place?

(A) It was difficult to start the fire.

(B) The fire took a long time to go out.

(C) They had to chop the wood into pieces.

(D) Ashes and smoke formed during the fire.

15. Lisette observes that a substance has a definite shape and volume. What is Lisette **most likely** to do to change the state of the substance?

(A) place the substance in a dark closet

(B) place the substance in the freezer

(C) place the substance in a high location

(D) place the substance in a warm oven

16. Declan mixed lemon juice, water, and sugar in a large pitcher. He stirred until the sugar was dissolved. What type of mixture did Declan make?

(A) solution

(B) property

(C) separation

(D) condensation

17. Tam wanted to separate the salt from salt water. Which of the following is the **best** option?

(A) allow the water to condense on a cold object

(B) allow the water to evaporate

(C) freeze the salt water

(D) keep the water at a constant temperature

18. A substance has a definite volume but takes the shape of its container. A student heats the substance. The substance expands, filling the container. Which change of state did the student **most likely** observe?

(A) a change from a liquid to a gas

(B) a change from a solid to a liquid

(C) a change from a liquid to a solid

(D) a change from a gas to a liquid

Apply Inquiry and Review the Big Idea

Write the answers to these questions.

19. Paper clips, salt, and gravel are mixed in a pile. Tasha wants to separate the parts of this mixture. What should she do to separate all three parts?

_____

_____

_____

20. Isabella pours juice into paper cups and places the cups in the freezer.

3 hours later

Describe the state change that happens inside the freezer.

_____

_____

21. Robert does an investigation using baking soda and vinegar.

a. What are the physical properties of the baking soda and the vinegar before Robert combines them?

_____

_____

b. What kind of change will Robert observe?

_____

c. How will Robert know this type of change took place?

_____

_____

Simple and Compound Machines

Big Idea

Simple machines make work easier to do by changing the direction or size of a force.

fishing with simple machines

I Wonder Why

Why does a fishing pole use a reel?
Turn the page to find out.

Here's why A fishing reel is a wheel-and-axle that helps pull in a heavy fish.

In this unit, you will explore the Big Idea, the Essential Questions, and the Investigations on the Inquiry Flipchart.

Levels of Inquiry Key ■ DIRECTED ■ GUIDED ■ INDEPENDENT

Track Your Progress

Big Idea Simple machines make work easier to do by changing the direction or size of a force.

Essential Questions

Now I Get the Big Idea!

Science Notebook

Before you begin each lesson, be sure to write your thoughts about the Essential Question.

Essential Question

What Are Simple Machines?

Engage Your Brain!

Find the answer to the following question in this lesson and record it here.

How is the rake helping the boy do work?

_____

_____

_____

_____

Active Reading

Lesson Vocabulary

List the terms. As you learn about each one, make notes in the Interactive Glossary.

_____   _____

_____   _____

_____   _____

Cause and Effect

Some ideas in this lesson are connected by a cause-and-effect relationship. Why something happens is a cause. What happens as a result of something else is an effect. Active readers look for effects by asking themselves, What happened? They look for causes by asking, Why did it happen?

403

How Can We Use Simple Machines?

Digging a hole in the sand. Moving a wagonload of toys. Whew! These jobs are work. Simple machines are useful because they make work easier.

Active Reading As you read these two pages, circle an everyday word that has a different meaning in science.

This shovel handle is a simple machine. It helps the boy lift sand more easily than he could on his own.

This girl is using a wagon to do the work of moving things. The handle of the wagon is a simple machine called a wheel-and-axle. It helps her steer and turn the wagon.

Think of the work you do each day. You do schoolwork. You may do other jobs at home, too. By bedtime, you may feel like you've put in a full day's work. Scientists define work in a specific way. **Work** is the use of a force—a push or a pull—to move an object in the same direction as the force.

The children on these pages are using simple machines to help them do work. A **simple machine** is something that makes work easier. A simple machine has few or no moving parts. To use it, you apply only one force.

Simple Machines

Look at the shovels below. Why are these shovel handles simple machines?

_____

_____

_____

_____

Levers Help You Lift

Levers are simple machines. They are often used to lift things. You use levers all the time without realizing it. How do they work?

Active Reading As you read these two pages, find and underline the definitions of *lever* and *fulcrum*.

A **lever** is a bar that pivots, or turns, on a fixed point. A fixed point is a point that doesn't move. The fixed point on a lever is called the **fulcrum** [FUHL•kruhm]. The load—what you are moving—is on one end of the lever. As you move the other end of the lever, the lever moves the load.

A fork is one kind of lever. The boy's thumb is the fulcrum. As he lowers his hand, the fork lifts the food—the load—to his mouth.

Lever

Output

Fulcrum

A seesaw is a lever. Its fulcrum is in the middle. The fulcrum is the object on which the seesaw sits. If your friend sits on one end of a seesaw, where would you apply force to lift her? You would sit on the other end of the seesaw.

Rakes and brooms are another type of lever. Your hands move when you rake leaves or sweep a floor, but the leaves or dirt—the load—moves farther than your hands do. This makes your job easier.

The Parts of a Lever

Draw a lever. Label the fulcrum, the load, and the applied force.

On a seesaw, you may be a load or a force. When you are coming down, your weight is the applied force. It presses down on one end of the lever and the load on the other side goes up. Then you trade. You are the load being lifted, and your partner's weight is the force.

Using a Wheel-and-Axle

Some simple machines use circular motion to make work easier.

Active Reading As you read these two pages, underline the phrases that describe the effect of turning each wheel-and-axle.

A **wheel-and-axle** is made up of a wheel and an axle that are connected so that they turn together. A wheel-and-axle uses a circular motion to increase force. If you turn the wheel, the axle turns with greater force.

Turning the handlebar is like turning the purple wheel. The connected axle turns to steer the front bicycle wheel.

Wheel

Axle

Look at the picture of the bicycle. The handlebars are connected to a shaft. Together, these act as a wheel-and-axle. When you turn the handlebars, the shaft, or axle, turns with it. Since the axle is connected to the front wheel, the wheel also turns. In this way, you can steer without having to turn the wheel from side to side with your hands.

The wheels and axles at the bottom of the bicycle are not true wheel-and-axles. These wheels turn on their axles. The axles do not turn with the wheels.

Another Wheel-and-Axle

A doorknob is another example of a wheel-and-axle. When you turn the knob, the axle turns, too. As it does, it pulls back the catch, and the door opens. Which part of the doorknob is the wheel?

A pencil sharpener has a wheel-and-axle. When you turn the crank, the axle carries the movement to the sharpener. It turns to sharpen the pencil.

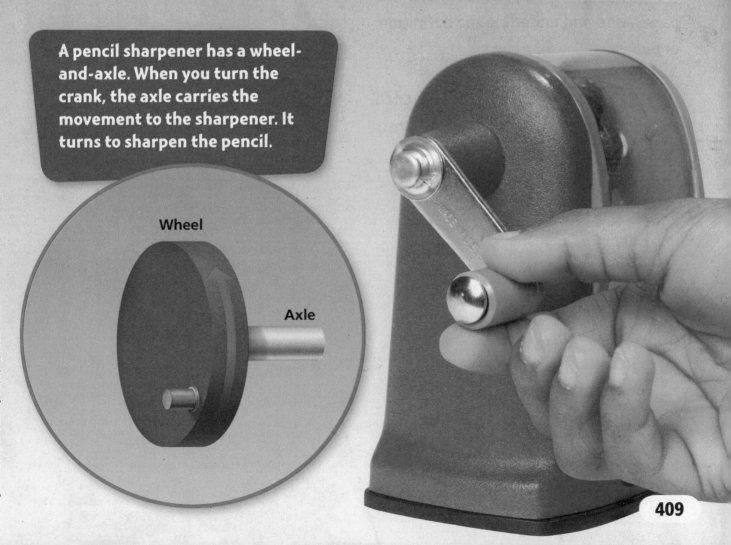

Wheel

Axle

Pulley Power

Going up! Coming down! You can use a simple machine, like a pulley, to lift a load straight up into the air.

Active Reading As you read these two pages, find and underline the definition of *pulley*.

A pulley is a wheel with a rope, cord, or chain around it. One end of the rope hangs on each side of the pulley. You can pull from the side, like the girls in the tree house.

The pulley is attached to the tree house. One end of the rope is in the tree house. The other end is attached to the basket. By pulling on the free end of the rope, the girls in the tree house raise the basket to their level.

Single pulley

effort

output

You can also pull from below, like the girl in the sailboat. She doesn't have to climb to the top of the pole to raise the sail. Instead, she simply pulls down on the rope. In both of these examples, the pulley changes the direction of the force that is applied to the rope.

A pulley lets you stay in one place and still use your force. It lets you pull up something that is too far down to reach, like the basket on the ground. And it lets you pull up something to a point too high to reach, like the sail.

The pulley is attached to the top of the mast of the sailboat. It can be used to raise and lower the sail. Look around your school. Check the windows and the gym. Where can you find pulleys?

pulley

Do the Math!
Solve a Word Problem

Karen could lift 18 pounds with a pulley. When Marcus helped her, they could lift 32 pounds. When Antonio also helped, they could lift 19 more pounds than that.

How many more pounds could Marcus and Karen lift than Karen could lift alone?

_____

_____

How many pounds could the three children lift all together?

_____

_____

When you're done, use the answer key to check and revise your work.

Write the term or terms that match each picture and caption.

1

_____

This involves using force to move an object across a distance.

2

_____

This fishing rod and reel is made of two simple machines.

3

_____

You can use this simple machine to help you lift sand.

4

_____

When you turn the doorknob, the latch opens.

5

_____

The lever balances on this.

Answer Key: 1. work 2. wheel-and-axle and lever 3. lever 4. wheel-and-axle 5. fulcrum

Name _____

Word Play

1 In each box, use vocabulary terms to describe the simple machines from this lesson.

simple machines

pulley*   work*

lever*   wheel-and-axle*

fulcrum*   *Key Lesson Vocabulary

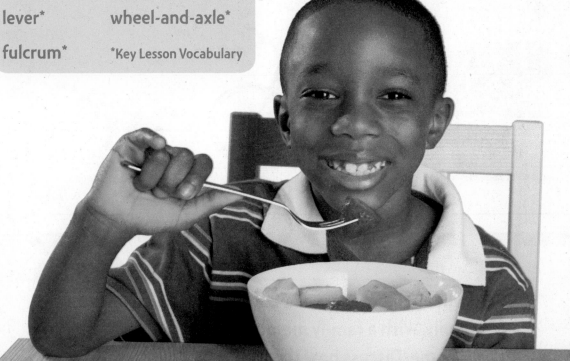

Apply Concepts

2 Make a list of simple machines in your school. Tell which type of simple machine each is.

_____

_____

_____

_____

3 Label each simple machine.

_____   _____   _____   _____

_____   _____   _____

Take It Home!

Share what you have learned about simple machines with your family. With a family member, identify simple machines in your home. Discuss how they make work easier.

Reach for the Sky:
Building with Cranes

All cranes have levers and pulleys. Cranes lift and lower heavy loads. People use cranes to make tall buildings. Follow the timeline to see how cranes have changed over time.

2,500 Years Ago

Cranes were first used in ancient Greece. They were used to build huge marble temples.

1800s

Steam engines were added to cranes. These cranes could move more easily and lift heavier loads.

Cranes were made out of steel. They had gas or electric engines and could lift much heavier loads.

1900s

What is the same about all the cranes?

_____

_____

Compare and Contrast

Review the cranes pictured and discussed in the timeline. Then answer the questions below.

Cranes lift beams to make the frame of a skyscraper.

2010

Today, skyscrapers are made using tower cranes. These giant cranes are made of steel. They can lift the heaviest loads. They are put together by smaller cranes, and the giant cranes can't move from place to place.

Choose any two cranes from the timeline. What is better about each newer crane? How did the design change? Give a possible reason for the change.

_____

_____

_____

Build On It!

Rise to the engineering design challenge—complete **Design It: Working Elevator Model** on the Inquiry Flipchart.

Essential Question

What Are Some Other Simple Machines?

Engage Your Brain!

Find the answer to the following question in this lesson and record it here.

The skateboarder looks like she's simply having fun, but she's also doing work. What work is being done? Which simple machine is she using?

_____

_____

_____

Active Reading

Lesson Vocabulary

List the terms. As you learn about each one, make notes in the Interactive Glossary.

_____ _____

_____

_____

Signal Words: Comparison

Signal words show connections between ideas. Words that signal comparisons, or similarities, include *like*, *same as*, *similar to*, and *resembles*. Active readers remember what they read because they are alert to signal words that identify comparisons.

Moving Up, Digging In

Simple machines are parts of tools we use every day. A ramp? It's a simple machine. A knife? It's another kind of simple machine. How do these simple machines work?

Active Reading As you read these two pages, find and underline the definitions of *inclined plane* and *wedge*.

A plane is a flat object, such as a board. An **inclined plane** is a plane that is slanted, so that one end is higher than the other. This makes it easier to lift a load. Instead of lifting the load straight up all at once, you push or pull it up the inclined plane, little by little. This spreads the work over a distance. Because of this, you are able to use less force.

It takes longer to roll a wheelchair up a ramp than to lift it. But lifting a wheelchair takes more effort. Raising the wheelchair with the ramp takes less effort because you apply a smaller force over a greater distance. You do the same amount of work, but the work is easier.

Inclined Plane

A **wedge** is two inclined planes placed back to back. One edge is sharp and pointed. The other is wide and flat. If you apply force to the flat edge, the pointed edge can split one thing into two things.

A knife is a wedge. The sharp edge of the knife opens a tiny crack. The inclined planes on either side push outward, widening the crack and separating the pieces as the wedge moves downward. The sharper the knife, the less effort is needed to get the work done.

Do the Math!
Calculate Force

An inclined plane that is 4 meters long and 2 meters high reduces the force needed to lift an object by one half. A person must use 90 units of force to lift an object straight up. How much force must the person use to push the object up this inclined plane?

_____

Wedge

When you use a knife to cut, the blade splits the food into two pieces.

419

All Wrapped Up

A wheel-and-axle uses circular motion to do work, but so does another simple machine—the screw.

Active Reading As you read these two pages, draw a box around each word that signals a comparison.

A screwdriver is a wheel-and-axle. It uses circular motion to make work easier. The tip of the screwdriver fits into the slot at the top of a screw. A **screw** is an inclined plane wrapped around a shaft or a cylinder. When you turn the screwdriver's handle, its shaft works like an axle to turn the screw. A screwdriver doesn't just turn the screw. Like other wheel-and-axles, the screwdriver takes your effort and increases that effort as it turns the screw.

As the screwdriver turns the screw, the inclined plane on the screw pulls it into the wood. The threads also make it hard to pull the screw out of the wood.

The thread around the screw is an inclined plane. This inclined plane is not straight like a ramp. It spirals around the screw.

Unlike a nail, which goes straight into the wood, a screw moves around and around as it goes in. As a result, it takes longer to insert a screw into the wood than it does a nail. But you use less force to get the screw into the wood. The closer together the threads are, the easier it is to turn the screw.

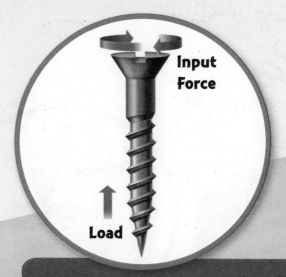

Input Force

Load

This man is using an ice auger [AW•ger]. As he turns the handle, the auger pulls the ice beneath it up to the surface. The ice is the load. As it moves up, a hole is made in the ice.

What Does a Screw Do?

Circle the screw in each picture. How does the screw help to do work?

_____

_____

_____

How Can Simple Machines Work Together?

Sometimes, two simple machines work together to get a job done. Which machines work this way?

Active Reading As you read these two pages, draw one line under a cause. Draw two lines under the effect.

Lever

Fulcrum

Wedge

The blades of these garden clippers are wedges, and the handles are levers.

© Houghton Mifflin Harcourt Publishing Company ©Stockbyte/Getty Images

Simple Machine	Description
Lever	Uses force at one end to move a load at the other end
Inclined Plane	Lets you lift a load using a smaller force over a greater distance
Screw	Uses an inclined plane wrapped around a post to move things up
Wedge	Lets you move two things apart or split one thing into two
Wheel-and-axle	Uses circular motion to increase force
Pulley	Uses a wheel and rope to change the size or direction of a force

A **compound machine** is a machine made up of two or more simple machines. Garden clippers are a compound machine. Bicycles are also compound machines. The handlebars are not the only wheel-and-axle on a bicycle. When you push down on the pedals, a wheel-and axle pulls the chain. This moves the bicycle forward.

Simple and Compound Machines

Look at the photos on this page. Tell which simple machines make up each compound machine.

_____

_____

_____

Why It Matters

Using Machines

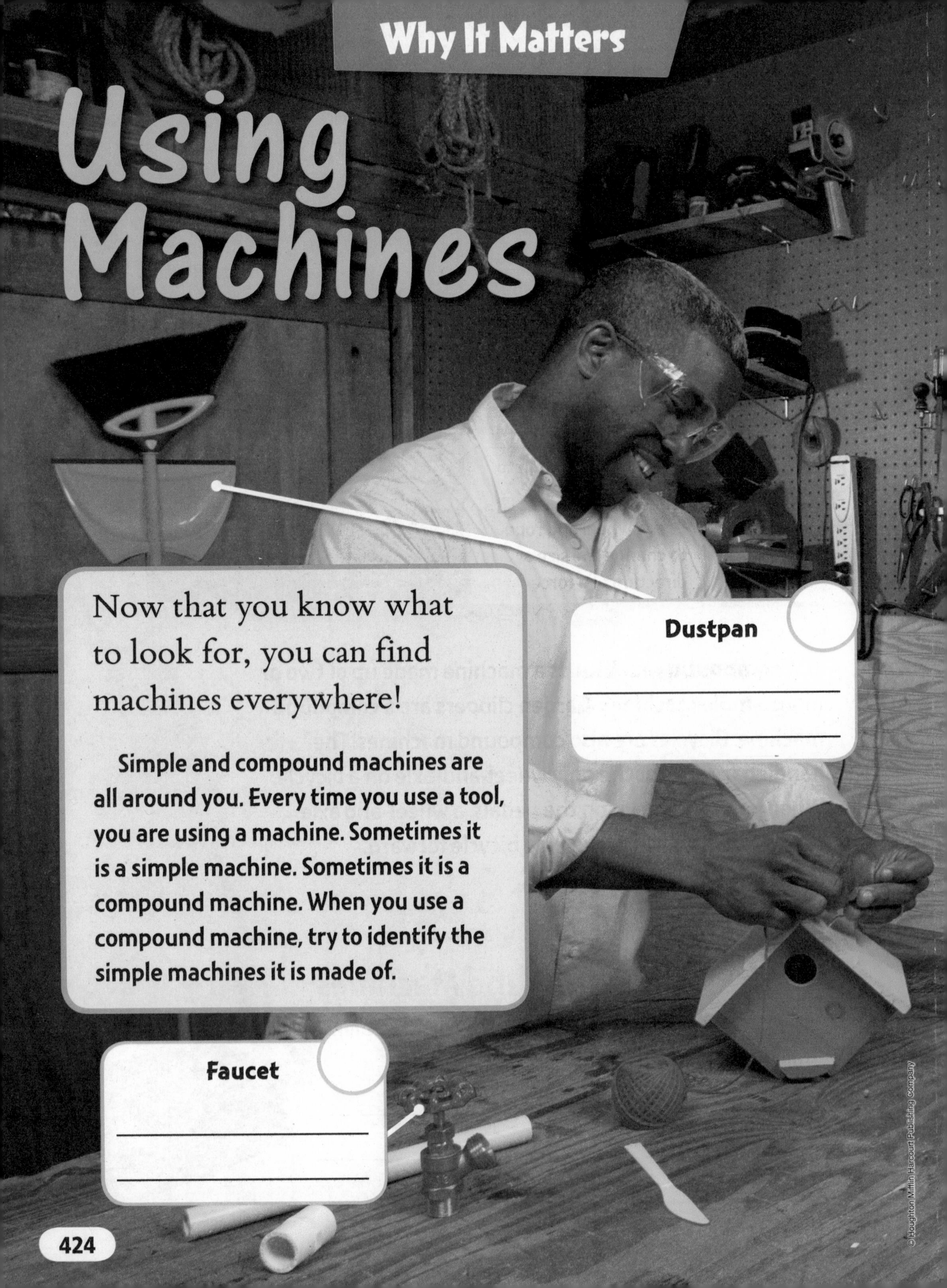

Dustpan
Faucet

Now that you know what to look for, you can find machines everywhere!

Simple and compound machines are all around you. Every time you use a tool, you are using a machine. Sometimes it is a simple machine. Sometimes it is a compound machine. When you use a compound machine, try to identify the simple machines it is made of.

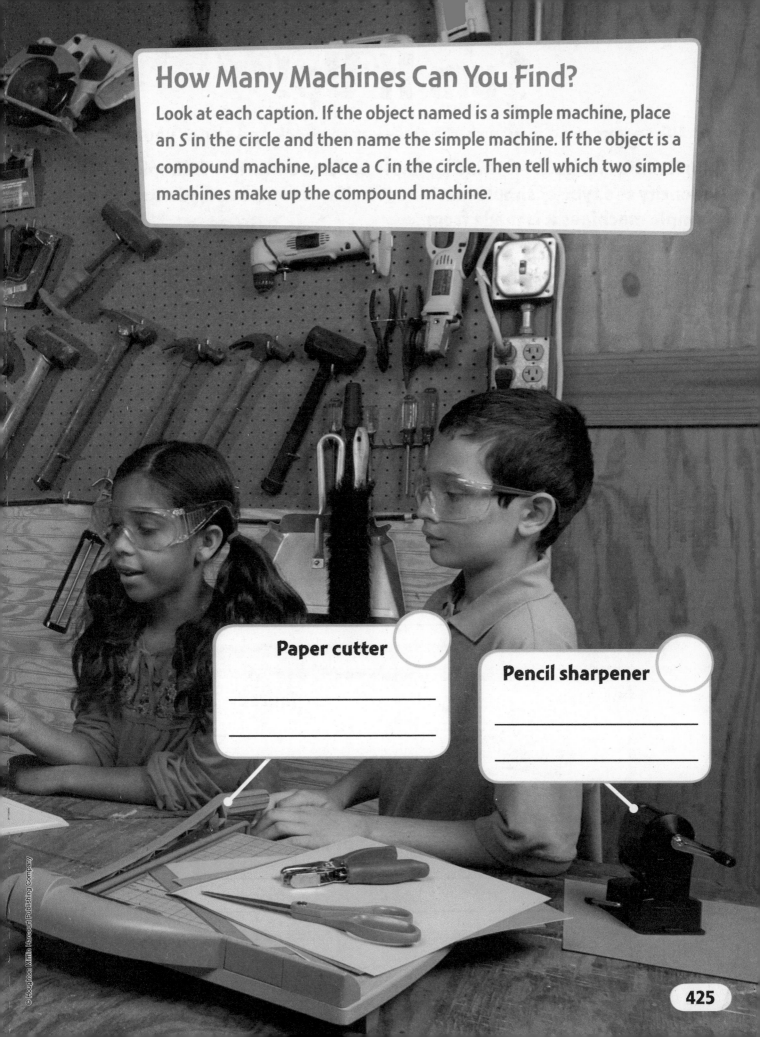

How Many Machines Can You Find?

Look at each caption. If the object named is a simple machine, place an *S* in the circle and then name the simple machine. If the object is a compound machine, place a *C* in the circle. Then tell which two simple machines make up the compound machine.

Paper cutter

_____
_____

Pencil sharpener

_____
_____

Sum It Up!

When you're done, use the answer key to check and revise your work.

Write whether each machine is simple or compound. If it is simple, identify the type of simple machine it is. If it is compound, identify the simple machines it is made from.

1 scissors
_____
_____

2 hatchet
_____
_____

3 screwdriver
_____
_____

4 faucet
_____
_____

5 pliers
_____
_____

Name _____

Word Play

1 Use the words in the box to complete the two concept webs about machines.

screw*	inclined plane*	paper cutter	scissors	rake
wedge*	compound machine*	screwdriver	bicycle	

* Key Lesson Vocabulary

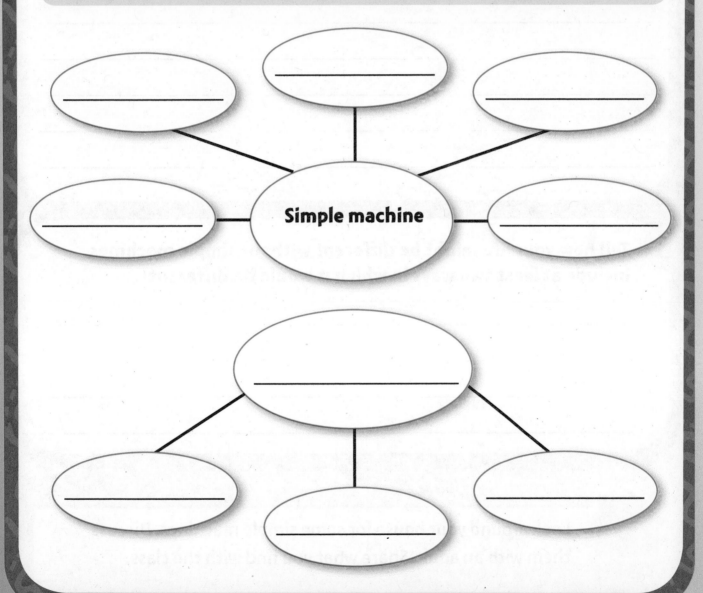

Apply Concepts

2 Identify each simple machine, and tell how you could use it.

Machine 1

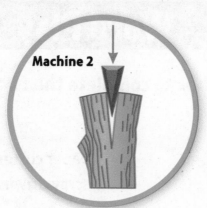

Machine 2

Machine 3

_____   _____   _____

_____   _____   _____

_____   _____   _____

_____   _____   _____

_____   _____   _____

3 Tell how your life might be different without simple machines. Include at least two ways in which it would be different.

_____

_____

_____

_____

Take It Home!

Look around your house for some simple machines. Discuss them with an adult. Share what you find with the class.

Inquiry Flipchart page 50

Lesson 3
INQUIRY

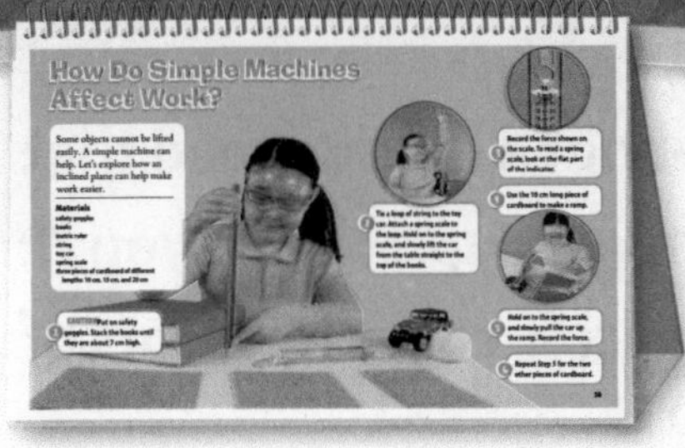

Name ______________________

Essential Question

How Do Simple Machines Affect Work?

Set a Purpose

What will you learn from this experiment?

____

____

____

Think About the Procedure

How do you think the spring scale measures force?

____

____

Why do you think you are using ramps of different lengths?

____

____

____

Record Your Data

Write your measurements in the table below.

Setup	Measurements
Without ramp	
With 10-cm ramp	
With 15-cm ramp	
With 20-cm ramp	

Draw Conclusions

Which moved the car a shorter distance: lifting straight up or using a ramp?

_____

_____

_____

Which was easier: lifting straight up or using a ramp?

_____

_____

_____

On which ramp did you use the least amount of force to move the car? Why do you think this was so?

_____

_____

_____

_____

Analyze and Extend

1. Why do you think an inclined plane makes it easier to lift objects?

_____

_____

_____

2. Think about a hillside road that goes straight up. Why do you think many hillside roads have lots of curves?

_____

_____

_____

_____

3. People living in ancient times built pyramids and other structures without the machines we have today. How do you think they were able to move heavy loads to the tops of the pyramids?

_____

_____

_____

_____

4. What other questions do you have about how simple machines affect work?

_____

_____

_____

_____

Meet the Machine Engineers

Helen Greiner 1967–

Imagine a robot in every home. That's what Helen Greiner says is the future. She is a roboticist. As a young girl, she loved science and machines. Greiner started a company to build robots. Now she designs and builds robots that can be used in homes. From toys to vacuum cleaners, she creates robots that make a difference in everyday lives.

One of Greiner's tiny robots explored the tunnels in the Great Pyramid of Giza in Egypt.

Dean Kamen 1951–

Dean Kamen is an inventor of very useful machines. One of his famous inventions is the Segway Human Transporter. When riding a Segway, people use their body weight to both balance and steer the machine. Kamen also started a group that holds special events to get students interested in technology.

The Segway is a two-wheeled personal transportation machine that runs on batteries.

Machines!

Read each clue and write the answer in the correct squares.

| Greiner | home | robot | Segway | technology |

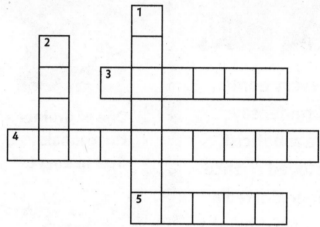

ACROSS

3. A _____ is a two-wheeled machine you can ride.

4. Kamen helps students get interested in _____.

5. A tiny _____ explored inside a pyramid.

DOWN

1. _____ is a roboticist.

2. Greiner wants every one of these to have a robot. _____

Unit 10 Review

Name _____

Vocabulary Review

Use the terms in the box to complete the sentences.

> compound machine
> fulcrum
> inclined plane
> wedge
> work

1. When you push a heavy box up a ramp, you are using a(n) _____.

2. An object with two or more simple machines combined is a(n) _____.

3. The object that supports a lever is a(n) _____.

4. When you use force to move an object, you are doing _____.

5. Two inclined planes placed together that make an edge form a(n) _____.

Science Concepts

Fill in the letter of the choice that best answers the question.

6. Heather uses an ax to chop wood for a campfire. The sharp tip of the ax makes a small cut in the wood. The cut gets larger as the wider part of the blade sinks into it. What type of simple machine is the tip of the ax?

   Ⓐ a pulley

   Ⓑ a wedge

   Ⓒ a fulcrum

   Ⓓ a wheel-and-axle

7. The picture shows a compound machine found in most homes and schools.

   Identify the two simple machines that work together to make the compound machine shown.

   Ⓐ wedge and lever

   Ⓑ inclined plane and wedge

   Ⓒ wheel-and-axle and lever

   Ⓓ wheel-and-axle and inclined plane

Science Concepts

Fill in the letter of the choice that best answers the question.

8. Jorge wants to load his piano onto a moving truck. He thinks that using a simple machine to spread the work over a longer distance would be a good idea. Which simple machine would be the **best** option?

    (A) screw

    (B) wedge

    (C) inclined plane

    (D) wheel-and-axle

9. Which of the following simple machines would be **best** for lifting cleaning supplies straight up the side of a tall building?

    (A) lever

    (B) pulley

    (C) inclined plane

    (D) wheel-and-axle

10. Taran wants to lift an object using a simple machine. The pictures show three possible ways he could set up the simple machine.

    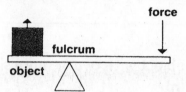

    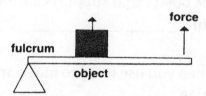

    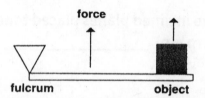

    Which picture or pictures show how Taran can use the simple machine so it would reduce the effort needed to lift the object?

    (A) the top picture

    (B) the middle picture

    (C) the bottom picture

    (D) the top and middle pictures

11. The picture shows one way a simple machine can be used.

What provides the force needed to pull the nail out of the board?

Ⓐ the hammer's head

Ⓑ the hammer's handle

Ⓒ the board's flat surface

Ⓓ the person's arm and hand

12. A 3 m ramp and a 5 m ramp are both used to wheel boxes of vegetables into a restaurant. Both ramps have one end on the ground and one end on the top step of the restaurant. Which statement **best** compares the ramps?

Ⓐ It takes less effort to wheel boxes up the 5 m ramp, but the distance is greater.

Ⓑ It takes less effort to wheel boxes up the 3 m ramp, but the distance is shorter.

Ⓒ It takes more effort to wheel boxes up the 5 m ramp, but the distance is shorter.

Ⓓ It takes more effort to wheel boxes up the 3 m ramp, but the distance is greater.

13. The picture shows a common example of a simple machine.

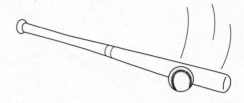

Tina uses the bat to hit the ball. What acts as the fulcrum?

Ⓐ the ball

Ⓑ the bat handle

Ⓒ Tina's hands

Ⓓ the thick part of the bat

14. What is one advantage of a wheel-and-axle?

Ⓐ You can lift a heavy load straight up.

Ⓑ You can turn a wheel without touching it.

Ⓒ You can use it to cut into a hard substance.

Ⓓ You can use less force to push or pull a load over a greater distance.

Apply Inquiry and Review the Big Idea

Write the answers to these questions.

15. Jacob did an experiment. He set up two ramps, shown below.

Predict what Jacob will find when he measures the force needed to pull the toy up each ramp.

_____

_____

_____

16. The tool shown in the picture is a compound machine.

Identify the simple machines, and explain how each one is used to make digging easier.

_____

_____

_____

17. Compare and contrast a screw and a wedge. How are they alike? How are they different?

_____

_____

_____

Interactive Glossary

As you learn about each term, add notes, drawings, or sentences in the extra space. This will help you remember what the terms mean. Here are some examples.

Fungi [FUHN•jeye] A kingdom of organisms that have a nucleus and get nutrients by decomposing other organisms

 A mushroom is from the kingdom Fungi.

physical change [FIHZ•ih•kuhl CHAYNJ] Change in the size, shape, or state of matter with no new substance being formed

When I cut paper, the paper has a physical change.

Glossary Pronunciation Key

With every glossary term, there is also a phonetic respelling. A phonetic respelling writes the word the way it sounds, which can help you pronounce new or unfamiliar words. Use this key to help you understand the respellings.

Sound	As in	Phonetic Respelling	Sound	As in	Phonetic Respelling
a	bat	(BAT)	oh	over	(OH•ver)
ah	lock	(LAHK)	oo	pool	(POOL)
air	rare	(RAIR)	ow	out	(OWT)
ar	argue	(AR•gyoo)	oy	foil	(FOYL)
aw	law	(LAW)	s	cell	(SEL)
ay	face	(FAYS)		sit	(SIT)
ch	chapel	(CHAP•uhl)	sh	sheep	(SHEEP)
e	test	(TEST)	th	that	(THAT)
	metric	(MEH•trik)		thin	(THIN)
ee	eat	(EET)	u	pull	(PUL)
	feet	(FEET)	uh	medal	(MED•uhl)
	ski	(SKEE)		talent	(TAL•uhnt)
er	paper	(PAY•per)		pencil	(PEN•suhl)
	fern	(FERN)		onion	(UHN•yuhn)
eye	idea	(eye•DEE•uh)		playful	(PLAY•fuhl)
i	bit	(BIT)		dull	(DUHL)
ing	going	(GOH•ing)	y	yes	(YES)
k	card	(KARD)		ripe	(RYP)
	kite	(KYT)	z	bags	(BAGZ)
ngk	bank	(BANGK)	zh	treasure	(TREZH•er)

Interactive Glossary

A

adaptation [ad•uhp•TAY•shuhn] Trait or characteristic that helps an organism survive (p. 116)

atmosphere [AT•muhs•feer] The layer of gases that surround Earth (p. 304)

axis [AK•sis] The imaginary line around which Earth rotates (p. 327)

B

bar graph [BAHR GRAF] A graph using parallel bars of varying lengths to show comparison (p. 37)

behavior [bih•HAYV•yer] The way an organism usually acts in a certain situation (p. 132)

C

camouflage [KAM•uh•flazh] The coloring, marking, or other physical appearance of an organism that helps it blend in with its surroundings (p. 120)

canyon [KAN•yuhn] A valley with steep sides (p. 206)

chart [CHART] A display that organizes data into rows and columns (p. 37)

chemical change [KEM•ih•kuhl CHAYNJ] A change in one or more substances that forms new and different substances (p. 386)

condensation [kahn•duhn•SAY•shuhn] The process by which a gas changes into a liquid (pp. 294, 373)

clay [KLAY] The smallest particles of rock that make up soil (p. 270)

cone [KOHN] A part of some nonflowering plants where seeds form (p. 93)

community [kuh•MYOO•nih•tee] All the populations of organisms that live and interact in an area (p. 154)

conservation [kahn•ser•VAY•shuhn] The use of less of something to make its supply last longer (p. 253)

compound machine [(KOM•pound muh•SHEEN] A machine that is made up of two or more simple machines (p. 423)

consumer [kuhn•SOOM•er] A living thing that cannot make its own food and must eat other living things (p. 170)

Interactive Glossary

D

data [DEY•tuh] Individual facts, statistics, and items of information (p. 35)

data table [DEY•tuh TEY•buhl] A kind of chart used for recording number data (p. 37)

decomposer [dee•kuhm•POHZ•er] A living thing that gets energy by breaking down dead organisms and animal wastes (p. 170)

design process [dih•ZYN PROS•es] The process of applying basic principles of engineering to solve problems (p. 56)

dissolve [di•ZOLV] To completely and evenly mix one substance in another (p. 383)

drought [DROUT] A long period of time with very little rain (p. 185)

E

earthquake [ERTH•kwayk] A shaking of Earth's surface that can cause land to rise and fall (p. 230)

ecosystem [EE•koh•sis•tuhm] A community of organisms and the physical environment in which they live (p. 152)

environment [en•vy•ruhn•muhnt] All the living and nonliving things that surround and affect an organism (p. 152)

experiment [ek•SPAIR•uh•muhnt] A test done to see whether a hypothesis is correct (p. 11)

erosion [uh•ROH•zhuhn] The process of moving weathered rock and soil from one place to another (pp. 184, 218)

F

flood [FLUD] A large amount of water that covers normally dry land (pp. 185, 234)

evaporation [ee•vap•uh•RAY•shuhn] The process by which a liquid changes into a gas (pp. 294, 372)

flower [FLOW•er] The part of a flowering plant that produces seeds (p. 92)

evidence [EV•uh•duhns] Data collected during an investigation (p. 35)

food chain [FOOD CHAYN] A series of organisms that depend on one another for food (p. 172)

Interactive Glossary

fossil fuel [FAHS•uhl FYOO•uhl] Fuel formed from the remains of once-living things. Coal, oil, and natural gas are fossil fuels. (p. 253)

germinate [JER•muh•nayt] To start to grow (a seed) (p. 92)

fresh water [FRESH WAW•ter] Water that has very little salt in it (p. 290)

glacier [GLAY•sher] A large, thick sheet of slow-moving ice (p. 218)

fulcrum [FUHL•kruhm] The balance point of a lever that supports the arm but does not move (p. 406)

graduated cylinder [GRAJ•oo•ay•tid SIL•in•der] A container marked with a graded scale used for measuring liquids (p. 21)

G

gas [GAS] The state of matter that does not have a definite shape or volume (p. 366)

H

habitat [HAB•ih•tat] The place where an organism lives and can find everything it needs to survive (p. 152)

hibernate [HY•ber•nayt] To go into a deep, sleeplike state for winter (p. 136)

infer [in•FER] To draw a conclusion about something (p. 6)

humus [HYOO•muhs] The remains of decayed plants or animals in the soil (p. 266)

instinct [IN•stinkt] An inherited behavior of an animal that helps it meet its needs (p. 132)

hypothesis [hy•PAHTH•uh•sis] A possible answer to a question that can be tested to see if it is correct (p. 10)

investigation [in•ves•tuh•GAY•shuhn] Procedure carried out to carefully observe, study, or test something in order to learn more about it (p. 9)

inclined plane [in•KLYND PLAYN] A simple machine that is a slanted surface (p. 418)

landform [LAND•fawrm] A natural shape or feature on Earth's surface (p. 205)

Interactive Glossary

larva [LAHR•vuh] The stage between egg and pupa in complete metamorphosis in insects (p. 107)

learned behavior [LERND bee•HAYV•yer] A behavior that an animal doesn't begin life with but develops as a result of experience or by observing other animals (p. 132)

lever [LEV•er] A simple machine made up of a bar that pivots, or turns, on a fixed point (p. 406)

life cycle [LYF SY•kuhl] The stages that a living thing passes through as it grows and changes (p. 92)

liquid [LIK•wid] The state of matter that has a definite volume but no definite shape (p. 366)

M

map [MAP] A picture that shows the locations of things (p. 37)

mass [MAS] The amount of matter in an object (p. 354)

matter [MAT•er] Anything that takes up space and has mass (p. 353)

metamorphosis [met•uh•MAWR•fuh•sis] A phase in the life cycle of many animals during which they undergo major changes in body form (p. 104)

mixture [MIKS•cher] A combination of two or more different substances that keep their identities (p. 382)

microscope [MY•kruh•skohp] A tool that makes an object look several times bigger than it is (p. 19)

model [MOD•l] A representation of something real that is too big, too small, or that has too many parts to be studied directly (p. 36)

migrate [MY•grayt] To travel from one place to another and back again (p. 138)

mountain [MOUNT•uhn] The highest kind of land, with sides that slope toward its top (p. 208)

mimicry [MIHM•ih•kree] An adaptation in which a harmless animal looks like an animal that is poisonous or that tastes bad, so that predators avoid it (p. 120)

N

natural resource [NACH•er•uhl REE•sawrs] Anything from nature that people can use (p. 250)

Interactive Glossary

nonrenewable resource
[nahn•rih•NOO•uh•buhl REE•sawrs] A resource that, once used, cannot be replaced in a reasonable amount of time (p. 253)

nutrients [NOO•tree•uhnts] Substances in soil that plants need to grow and stay healthy (p. 272)

O

observe [uhb•ZURV] To use your senses to gather information (p. 6)

oxygen [OK•si•jun] A gas in the air and water, which most living things need to survive (p. 304)

P

photosynthesis [foht•oh•SIHN•thuh•sis] The process in which plants use energy from the sun to change carbon dioxide and water into sugar and oxygen (p. 168)

physical change [FIHZ•ih•kuhl CHAYNJ] A change in which a new substance is not formed (p. 380)

physical property [FIHZ•ih•kuhl PRAHP•er•tee] A characteristic of matter that you can observe or measure directly (p. 353)

plain [PLAYN] Flat land that spreads out a long way (p. 210)

plateau [pla•TOH] A flat area higher than the land around it (p. 210)

population [pahp•yuh•LAY•shuhn] All the organisms of the same kind that live together in an ecosystem (p. 154)

pollen [POL•uhn] A powder-like material that plants need to make seeds (p. 94)

precipitation [pri•sip•uh•TAY•shuhn] Water that falls from clouds to Earth's surface (p. 296)

pollination [pol•uh•NEY•shuhn] The transfer of pollen from the male structures to the female structures of seed plants (p. 94)

predict [pri•DIKT] Use observations and data to form an idea of what will happen under certain conditions (p. 8)

pollution [puh•LOO•shuhn] Any harmful substance in the environment (p. 256)

producer [pruh•DOOS•er] A living thing, such as a plant, that can make its own food (p. 168)

Interactive Glossary

pulley [PUHL•ee] A simple machine made of a wheel with a rope, cord, or chain around it (p. 410)

revolution [rev•uh•LOO•shuhn] The movement of Earth one time around the sun (p. 328)

pupa [PYOO•puh] The stage of complete metamorphosis in which an insect changes from a larva to an adult (p. 107)

rotation [ro•TAY•shuhn] The turning of Earth on its axis (p. 327)

renewable resource [rih•NOO•uh•buhl REE•sawrs] A resource that can be replaced within a reasonable amount of time (p. 250)

salt water [SAWLT WAW•ter] Water found in oceans and seas; makes up 97% of Earth's water (p. 290)

reproduce [ree•pruh•DOOS] To make more living things of the same kind (p. 92)

sand [SAND] The largest particles of rock that make up soil (p. 270)

screw [SKROO] A simple machine made of a post with an inclined plane wrapped around it (p. 420)

solid [SAHL•id] The state of matter that has a definite volume and shape (p. 366)

silt [SILT] Particles of rock that are smaller than sand but larger than clay (p. 270)

solution [suh•LOO•shuhn] A mixture in which all the parts are evenly mixed (p. 383)

simple machine [SIM•puhl muh•SHEEN] A machine with few or no moving parts that you apply just one force to (p. 405)

spore [SPAWR] A reproductive structure made by seedless plants, including mosses and ferns (p. 96)

soil [SOYL] A mixture of water, air, tiny pieces of rock, and humus (p. 266)

tadpole [TAD•pohl] A young frog that comes out of an egg and has gills to take in oxygen from the water (p. 105)

Interactive Glossary

technology [tek•NOL•uh•jee] Anything that people make or do that changes the natural world (p. 70)

variable [VAIR•ee•uh•buhl] The one thing that changes in an experiment (p. 11)

temperature [TEM•per•uh•cher] A measure of how hot or cold something is (pp. 23, 306, 358)

volcano [vahl•KAY•noh] A mountain made of lava, ash, or other materials from eruptions (p. 232)

tide [TYD] The regular rise and fall of the ocean's surface, caused mostly by the moon's gravitational pull on Earth's oceans (p. 334)

volume [VAHL•yoom] The amount of space that matter takes up (p. 356)

valley [VAL•ee] The low land between mountains or hills (p. 206)

water cycle [WAW•ter SY•kuhl] The movement of water from Earth's surface to the air and back again (p. 296)

weather [WEH•ther] What is happening in the atmosphere at a certain place and time (p. 304)

wheel-and-axle [WEEL AND AK•suhl] A simple machine made of a wheel and an axle that turn together (p. 408)

weathering [WETH•er•ing] The breaking down of rocks on Earth's surface into smaller pieces (p. 216)

work [WERK] The use of a force to move an object over a distance (p. 405)

wedge [WEJ] A simple machine composed of two inclined planes back to back (p. 419)

Index

condensation, 294–295, 373

cones, 93

conservation, 253, 258–259

consumers, 170–171

copper, 254, 364

coral, 279

corn, 174–175

cotton, 255

cranes, 415–416

crops, 174–175

crust of Earth, 204–205, 230, 232

cube, 356

cubic centimeters, 357

cumulus clouds, 305

data, 34–41
  evidence and, 34–35
  graphs and tables, 37–41
  recording and displaying, 36–39

data tables, 37–41

day-and-night cycle, 326–327

decomposers, 170–171

deltas, 220–221

desert ecosystems, 156

desert plants, 122

design process, 56–63
  cell phones, 62–63
  finding a problem, 58–59
  measurement and recording, 59
  planning and building, 60–61
  prototypes and, 60–61

dissolved substance, 383

diversity, 108–109

doorknob, 409

Do the Math!
  calculate force, 419
  estimate an answer, 95

estimate the difference, 209

find the fraction, 291

find the volume, 356

interpret a graph, 41, 187

interpret a table, 73

make a bar graph, 155

make a graph, 139

measure in millimeters, 107

read a table, 63

skip count by 5s, 235

solve a story problem, 259, 369

solve a two-step problem, 389

solve a word problem, 123, 175, 219, 307, 411

subtract units, 21

use a data table, 331

Draw Conclusions, 16, 30, 46, 68, 82, 114, 130, 164, 180, 228, 264, 316, 342, 378, 394, 430

drawing conclusions, 11

dropper, 18

drought, 185

Earth
  atmosphere of, 304–305
  axis of, 327
  crust of, 204–205, 230, 232
  earthquakes, 230–231
  erosion and, 184, 218–219
  fire and flood, 234
  landslides and mudslides, 235
  layers of, 204
  revolution of, 328–329
  rotation of, 326–327
  seasons of, 328–329
  volcanoes, 232–233
  weathering and, 216–217

earthquakes, 230–231, 241–242

earth scientists, 241–242

ecosystems, 152–159
  animals and plants in, 152–153, 186–187
  communities, 154–155
  fire in, 182–183, 234
  habitats, 152–153
  land, 156–157
  ocean, 152–153, 158
  populations, 154–155
  study of, 165–166
  water, 158–159, 184–185

electricity, 252

emergency planning, 236–237

energy
  fossil fuels, 253–255
  heat, 370–371
  natural resources and, 252–253
  solar cells, 255

Engineering and Technology. *See also* STEM (Science, Technology, Engineering, and Mathematics)
  cranes, 415–416
  erosion technology, 225–226
  firefighting, 195–196
  food preservation, 143–144
  natural resources, 395–396
  observatories, 343–344
  raincoats, 317–318
  recycling and pollution, 281–282

environment, 152
  animals and, 186
  people and, 188–191
  pollution, 188
  water and, 184–185

environmental scientists, 279–280

erosion, 184
  beach, 225
  plants and, 220

Index

Index

Index